PAYING FOR COLLEGE

Answers to All Your Questions About Financial Aid, Scholarships, Tuition Payment Plans, and Everything Else You Need to Know

PETERSON'S

A **nelnet** COMPANY

About Peterson's, a Nelnet company

Peterson's (www.petersons.com) is a leading provider of education information and advice, with books and online resources focusing on education search, test preparation, and financial aid. Its Web site offers searchable databases and interactive tools for contacting educational institutions, online practice tests and instruction, and planning tools for securing financial aid. Peterson's serves 110 million education consumers annually.

For more information, contact Peterson's, 2000 Lenox Drive, Lawrenceville, NJ 08648; 800-338-3282; or find us on the World Wide Web at www.petersons.com/about.

ISBN-13: 978-0-7689-2714-6
ISBN-10: 0-7689-2714-5

Printed in the United States of America

10 9 8 7 6 5 4 3 2 1   09 08 07

First Edition

ACKNOWLEDGMENTS

Special thanks to the following people for their assistance:

Don Betterton, former Director of Financial Aid, Princeton University

Dr. Lawrence Burt, Former Director, Student Financial Services, University of Texas Austin

Dr. Herm Davis, Executive Director of the National College Scholarship Foundation

Brenda Dillon, Vice President Federal Program Product Manager, Key Education Resources

Heather Domeier, Assistant Director of Student Financial Services, Rice University

Ellen Frishberg, Former Director of Financial Aid, Johns Hopkins

Audrey Hill, Professional School Counselor, Col. Zadok Magruder High School, Rockville, Maryland

Ron Johnson, Director of Financial Aid, UCLA

John Nametz, Director of Financial Aid, University of Arizona

Stephen D. Rouff, Associate Director of Financial Aid (retired), Rutgers University

Dr. Lawrence Waters, Dean of Admissions and Enrollment Services, Ball State University

Richard Woodland, former Director of Financial Aid, Rutgers University—Camden

Kathy Wyler, former Bursar, University of Wisconsin-Parkside

OTHER RECOMMENDED PETERSON'S TITLES:

Scholarships, Grants & Prizes

College Money Handbook

Four-Year Colleges

Master the SAT

The Real ACT Prep Guide

Vocab Rock: Musical Prep for the SAT & ACT

Parent's Guide to the SAT & ACT

CONTENTS

Contents

Contents

Contents

FOREWORD

Like a fingerprint, each family's financial situation is unique and no two financial aid applications are alike. There are many paths to follow in order to receive financial aid, and each family deserves individual assistance, service, and, most important, solutions. A college education is a significant family investment. Like any purchase—large or small—you want to get the most "bang for your buck." In order to achieve this, you need to be a smart consumer. Total cost of attendance at some private colleges can exceed $45,000 a year, including tuition, fees, and room and board, and costs have been going steadily upward. According to the American Association of State Colleges and Universities, the average annual increase at state schools is around 7 percent, and tuition increases at private colleges are averaging around 6 percent. Since you are literally competing against thousands of other families for limited funds, you must shop intelligently and arm yourself with solid knowledge. And today, more than in years past, families are looking at an increased gap between what they can afford to pay and what colleges are willing to offer.

A leading aid administrator says, "The thinking family takes owner-ship of the application, understands options, and creates 'best chances' for funding. The thinking parent understands school policies: where there is flexibility and where there isn't. This mindset will enhance the ability to choose appropriate avenues for action and to influence outcomes."

As a smart consumer, you need to compare the value of an institution versus your real out-of-pocket expenses, while taking into consideration the value the institution places on your child, as reflected in the aid package.

Ask yourself:

➤ Is a brand-name school worth a large family debt burden?

➤ Is the amount of unmet-need aid worth the degree?

➤ Is the institution guiding you, step-by-step, on funding solutions, or is it leaving it up to you to figure things out?

➤ Will grant aid increase with cost of attendance increases?

Peterson's Paying for College is your consumer guide to the college funding process. This book was created to alleviate your stress and worry and provide you with the information you need to make your search for financial aid as simple and successful as possible. Here you will find ideas, tips, experiences, and funding solutions to help your family get the most bang for its buck and discover valuable information about the various federal, state, and institutional aid programs. You will learn how a school's cost of attendance is defined and how your ability to contribute to your child's education costs is calculated. You will get strategies for filling the gaps between the cost of attendance and your resources as well as how to compare various financial aid packages. Further, it gives you some of the best questions to ask admissions and financial aid officers during your campus visits and offers the best tips from education professionals across the country. In the "If I Only Knew..." chapter, families who have been through the financial aid "game" tell you how to adapt and best use the financial aid system. But most of all, this book shows you how to anticipate what your next move should be. You can't just fill out a financial aid application, drop it in the mail or click "Send," and wait. If you do, you lose the competitive edge, and getting money for college is competitive.

Smart consumers know where to go to get the best deal. For college funding solutions, you need the right information and the right connection at the right time. This book is your personal connection to the resources available to finance your child's higher education. Remember, it's your money. Make sure you get the best deal and the best service.

1

Financial Aid: The Basics

FAST FACTS

➤ **Everyone should apply for financial aid.** There are so many different factors that determine aid eligibility that no one can give you a simple answer as to whether or not you are eligible for aid. Family income and assets are not the only aspects that determine eligibility for need-based aid; family size and number of children in college are almost as important.

➤ **Parents should make sure students are involved in and understand the financial aid process.** At most schools, the student is the first point of contact for administrative issues. Many times, the financial aid process is the first step that students take in learning to manage their own financial matters.

➤ **Make sure that learning more about financial aid is on your radar screen early.** Too often families put nearly all their effort into the admission process and treat financial aid as an afterthought. This is a mistake. Learn as much as you can about the aid policies and practices at the colleges your child is considering.

Paying for college can generate a lot of stress and worry for parents, especially when they take a look at the price tags of schools. As a result, some families do not encourage their children to go to college because they do not believe they can afford it. They also don't consider the more expensive schools because the high cost of tuition scares them off. Other families forego applying for financial aid because they think their family income is too high or that they have too much in savings. However, thanks to financial aid, not only is college affordable for all families, but most families qualify for enough aid to make even the most expensive school affordable.

> Talk with your child about your ability and willingness to pay for college. Keep the lines of communication open about finances. Be clear and realistic about your financial limitations as well as your expectations of the role your child will take in the process of applying to and financing college.

JUST SO I UNDERSTAND, FINANCIAL AID IS . . .

Financial aid is money that is supplied by outside sources to help pay for the cost of an education beyond high school. It is important to note that there are two basic categories of financial aid: non-need-based and need-based.

1. **Non-need-based aid is also known as merit-based aid.** It is generally given to students in recognition of special skills, talent, or academic ability. Qualifications for merit-based aid are usually competitive in nature, and recipients are chosen because of their abilities in whatever criteria are used for selection (e.g., musical talent or athletic ability). Non-need-based aid can also be awarded based on other criteria, such as field of study, community service, or leadership abilities.

2. **Need-based aid, however, constitutes the major portion of assistance available.** When a family does not have sufficient resources to pay for an education beyond high school, it is considered to have financial need. Having documented financial need is the primary requirement for receiving need-based

aid, although you and your child have to meet other eligibility criteria as well. Whether or not you have sufficient financial resources to meet the cost of attending a college is usually determined through the collection of financial data about your family and then analyzing that data according to a standard set of calculations. This need assessment, or need analysis, results in an Expected Family Contribution (EFC). The EFC represents the resources, in dollars, that a student's family is expected to contribute toward education expenses for a given academic year.

There are three basic types of need-based aid (note that students usually must maintain satisfactory academic progress to remain eligible for all three types of financial aid):

1. **Grants and scholarships don't need to be repaid or maintained by a job.** Grants are usually based on financial need alone, while scholarships are given to students who have met some criteria, such as academic or athletic merit, regardless of whether the student needs the money to help pay for college.

2. **Work-study allows students to work 10–15 hours per week during the academic year and full-time during the summer to earn money to help pay for educational expenses.**

3. **Loans are the most widely available sources of need-based aid.** You must repay them, but the interest rates for federal student loans are often lower than for commercial loans, and payments are usually deferred until after the student has completed college.

All financial aid monies, whether need-based or non-need-based, come from four sources: federal, state, institutional, and private. The federal government is the largest source of need-based aid, providing more than $90 billion in student aid each year. State-supported financial aid varies

Use the free EFC calculator at www.petersons.com/finaid to get a head start.

from state to state and may carry restrictions regarding residency in the state and/or attendance at a school within the state. Most colleges and universities provide need-based and non-need-based aid to their students. This type of aid is referred to as institutional aid and varies by school. Institutional aid is offered to National Merit Scholars, high-school valedictorians, minorities, siblings, first-generation college students, and many more. The importance of institutional aid has increased in recent years as education costs have increased. Private aid can be a significant help in meeting education costs and reducing debt. But typically, it requires the most work on the part of the student in terms of locating the sources of funding and applying for the aid.

In case you think your circumstances are unique, you may be surprised to learn that:

➢ 80 percent of full-time students receive some form of financial aid.

➢ Financial aid covers 40 percent or more of the budget for full-time students.

➢ 20 percent of undergraduates come from a family with an income below $20,000 a year.

WHY YOUR FAMILY SHOULD APPLY FOR FINANCIAL AID

Have a "financial" safety school. This is one you can afford no matter what. Having a financial safety school frees your child up to apply to schools that may seem to be out of range financially.

Here are the most common worries and concerns that parents have about applying for financial aid and why you shouldn't let these concerns stop you from submitting an aid application:

➢ **The application form requests too much personal information.** With pages and pages of forms to fill out, the financial aid process may seem intrusive and intimidating. In addition, you may feel reluctant to share private financial information when you don't know who'll be reading it. Once you get started, however, you'll soon find that the forms aren't as complicated as they seem and that the information requested is no more than what the IRS wants to know every year.

➤ **Financial aid is charity; I should be able to pay for my kids' education myself.** Just because you need financial aid doesn't mean that your income isn't up to snuff or that you've failed to take responsibility for your children—it's the rare family that can afford the high cost of college these days. The premise of financial aid is that students and parents should be responsible for paying for their own education, but they don't yet have the means; therefore, the government provides aid as an investment. A college degree usually means that the student will get a higher-paying job, contribute more to society, and pay more taxes over the course of his or her lifetime.

➤ **I don't want to take on a huge debt burden.** It's true that most families have to borrow money to pay for college. But an education loan is not like borrowing to pay for a vacation or credit card debt. It's a wise investment that should produce a good return—a professional career for your child. Also, education loans often carry lower interest rates and fewer penalties than consumer loans. Finally, keep in mind that some loans can be forgiven, and loan forgiveness programs, in areas such as teaching, nursing, and military service, are expanding each year.

➤ **Financial aid is so confusing; there's too much to learn and I'm bound to make mistakes.** The financial aid application process can be intimidating. Don't be afraid to seek out help and advice from the high school guidance office, your state's financial aid agency, and reliable Internet resources. The absolute best resources, though, are the financial aid officers at the colleges where your child is applying; they will explain the requirements for their schools and work with you when you go through the application process. During the campus visit, set up an appointment with an aid officer—you'll probably find afterward that you feel much more relaxed about applying for aid.

CHAPTER

Details, Details: Forms and Paperwork

FAST FACTS

➤ **Complete the FAFSA.** The Free Application for Federal Student Aid, commonly referred to as the FAFSA, is the primary document for establishing eligibility for need-based federal financial aid. It is frequently used for state financial aid and institutional scholarships as well. The FAFSA must be submitted each year after January 1.

➤ **Pay attention to deadlines.** Families who pay attention to deadlines have an advantage over those who don't. Even if you have to estimate your figures on your FAFSA or institutional applications, you should do so. The sooner you file your application, the better your chances of receiving aid. Also, you should file your income taxes as early in the year as possible.

➤ **Students and parents should register with the U.S. Department of Education for the purpose of securing Personal Identification Numbers (PINs).** This allows you to sign the FAFSA online and speeds up the processing of the FAFSA.

➤ **Keep copies of everything you use to complete forms when you apply for aid.** A school may ask for documentation to support the data you supply.

The process of applying for financial aid can be quite lengthy, and some funds, particularly grant funds, are limited. Submit all required application and follow-up forms according to the schools' deadline to ensure being considered for all available funds and to receive timely notification of the funds being offered. Never wait until an admission offer has been made before applying for financial aid. Waiting is the surest way to miss out on the best financial aid package!

THE NEED EQUATION

Need-based aid is the major portion of assistance available for higher education. When you don't have sufficient resources to pay for your child's education beyond high school, you are considered to have financial need. Although financial need is the main requirement for need-based aid, you must meet other eligibility criteria as well. To determine if you have sufficient financial resources to meet college costs, financial data is collected and analyzed according to a standard set of calculations. This need assessment, or need analysis as it is generally called, results in an Expected Family Contribution (EFC). The EFC represents the resources, in dollars, that a student and his or her family are expected to contribute toward education expenses for a given year.

For purposes of student financial aid, need is expressed as an equation, using two components:

Cost of Attendance (COA)

− Expected Family Contribution (EFC)

= Financial Need

The EFC is calculated through a process known as need analysis. The COA is determined by each individual school, so it varies. In general, the Cost of Attendance at any school includes the following items:

➢ Tuition and fees

➢ Room

➢ Board

> Books and supplies

> Transportation

> Personal expenses

A school may also include the costs associated with education loans, study abroad, the purchase of a personal computer, participation in a cooperative education program, and a disability, if applicable.

Schools that participate in the federal student aid programs are required to make certain types of information available to prospective students. You need to carefully examine the published costs to make sure they are realistic and to make sure those costs are reasonable for you given your child's eventual career goals.

The type of school your child chooses (public, private, vocational, trade, or technical; two-year or four-year; graduate/professional, local community college, or distant residential school) can have a significant influence on cost and also on the types and sources of aid available to help finance that cost. While costs may vary from school to school, the EFC usually does not. Generally speaking, financial need increases when the Cost of Attendance is higher.

THE FREE APPLICATION FOR FEDERAL STUDENT AID

The application form that all students must use to apply for most federal financial aid is called the Free Application for Federal Student Aid (FAFSA). The income, asset, and demographic information you provide on the six-page FAFSA serves as the basis for determining your child's eligibility for federal student aid programs and, in many cases, institutional, state, and private sources of aid.

You need to complete only one FAFSA, even if your child is applying for admission to more than one school. Keep in mind that you can use the FAFSA to request that application information be sent to as many as six different schools at a time. To designate where information should be sent, the school's complete name, address, and appropriate federal school code must be provided on the FAFSA. A list of federal school codes can be found at www.fafsa.ed.gov.

Paper FAFSAs can be printed from a PDF at www.fafsa.ed.gov. Students are notified each year to file the renewal FAFSA; if you provided an e-mail address on the FAFSA, you will be notified electronically. Be sure to check with your financial aid administrator or call 800-4-FED-AID if you do not receive information about the renewal FAFSA.

FAFSA on the Web

You can apply electronically for federal student aid by using FAFSA on the Web (www.fafsa.ed.gov). FAFSA on the Web is an Internet application developed by the Department of Education that can be used to complete an electronic FAFSA. A FAFSA filed on the Web is processed much faster than the paper application. Use a browser that has been certified for use with FAFSA on the Web so you don't encounter problems while entering your application that Customer Service can't resolve. By using an approved browser, you can complete and submit your FAFSA information directly to the Central Processing System (CPS). After transmitting an application over the Internet, you can either mail your printed and completed signature page to the FAFSA processor at the CPS to complete the application process, or you can electronically sign it by using a Personal Identification Number (PIN) obtained from the FAFSA Web site by clicking on "PIN site." You can also go directly to the PIN site at www.pin.ed.gov. It can take up to five days to receive a PIN via e-mail.

> About 80 percent of FAFSA filers now complete the FAFSA online.

Once the signature page is received, the CPS will mail a Student Aid Report (SAR) to you if you did not provide an e-mail address. If you did provide an e-mail address, a link to the SAR will be sent to the address provided.

The Student Aid Report

In response to filing the FAFSA, a Student Aid Report (SAR) or a SAR Information Acknowledgment is sent from the CPS. If you submitted a paper FAFSA directly to the FAFSA processor, used FAFSA Express, or used FAFSA on the Web, you will receive a SAR consisting of two parts. If you submitted a FAFSA directly to the school for electronic transmission to the CPS, you will receive a one-page, noncorrectable SAR Information Acknowledgment.

The SAR summarizes the application data you supplied on the FAFSA and provides information about the amount that you are expected to pay for your child's education costs in the upcoming year. The SAR also provides you with instructions about what to do next. For example, if you have a problem with your Social Security number, the SAR provides instructions about the steps that must be taken to correct the problem.

In most cases, you do not have to submit your SAR to the school your child plans to attend unless there are errors in the information reported on the SAR. It is important to understand that all schools must have an official EFC from the Central Processing System to make an award. Schools are able to obtain your official EFC electronically. This electronic output document is called an Institutional Student Information Record, or ISIR.

Tips for Filing Online

If you elect to file your FAFSA online and establish a PIN, you can:

> ➤ Sign your FAFSA electronically.

> ➤ Review and correct errors on your electronic SAR.

> ➤ Print a copy of your SAR.

> ➤ Electronically sign loan promissory notes.

> ➤ Reapply for student aid every year your child is in school.

> ➤ View information about federal loans and grants you've received.

Other advantages include:

> ➤ PINs don't expire.

> ➤ One PIN can be used to sign FAFSAs for multiple children attending college.

> ➤ If you forget your PIN, or if it gets lost, you can go to the PIN Web site (www.pin.ed.gov) and, after answering a few identifying questions, have your PIN recovered and sent to you.

Completing the FAFSA

In their rush to complete the FAFSA, families often make costly errors. Here are three of the biggest errors to avoid:

1. **Not filling out the FAFSA completely and accurately.** Incomplete or inaccurate information can cause delays in processing applications. Errors can also result in a reduction of the total aid offered to your child.

2. **Not submitting all of the required applications for all possible sources of aid.** For example, many schools require a supplemental application for institutional aid. Confirm, and reconfirm if necessary, that you have submitted all required

forms and that the appropriate individual or organization has received what they need.

3. **Not submitting application forms by the published priority filing dates.** Most schools require you to submit the FAFSA and other financial aid application documents by a priority filing date. Families that miss this date are frequently offered less financial aid or less desirable financial aid than they would have been offered otherwise.

It is important to understand that when applying for financial aid, you accept certain responsibilities. These responsibilities include providing correct, accurate, and timely information; reviewing and understanding the agreements contained on any of the forms you sign; complying with application deadlines and requests for additional information; and repaying any funds received as a result of inaccurate information.

Another responsibility is to check on the status of your application. If you applied online, you should check one week after submitting the application. If you mailed in your application, or filed electronically and mailed in a signature page, check 2–3 weeks after submitting the application.

> FAFSA changes every year, so check the Web for updates.

You can check the status of your application either by calling 800-4-FED-AID (toll-free) or via the Web at www.fafsa.ed.gov. Note that you can check the status via the Web site even if you mailed in your application. Anyone who checks their status online must have a PIN.

Where the Information Is Sent

When the FAFSA processor receives your completed paper FAFSA, your data is entered into a computer system and electronically transmitted to the CPS. The CPS analyzes your paper or electronic FAFSA and transmits the results of the application to you, the schools, and to your state's financial aid agency.

The SAR summarizes information reported on your FAFSA and displays your EFC. When you receive the SAR, either on paper or electronically, review the information you submitted, as reported on the SAR, to confirm that it is accurate.

At the same time that the SAR is sent to you, the CPS also electronically transmits an applicant's data and an analysis (the ISIR) to the school(s) you listed on the FAFSA. Schools use this information, usually in conjunction with other documents submitted, to determine eligibility for federal, institutional, and state aid. FAFSA information is also transmitted by the CPS to your state agency so that your child may be considered for any state-sponsored financial aid programs.

All schools now participate in the Department of Education's Electronic Data Exchange and receive your FAFSA information electronically, so you will probably not need to send them a copy of the SAR. Be sure to keep a copy of the SAR for your records, since it has certain information not available anywhere else. If the school does ask for a copy, send the most updated version.

If you are filing a paper FAFSA, you can indicate up to six schools to receive your information. You may add more schools to your record once your FAFSA is processed. There are three ways to do this:

1. **If you have a PIN, go to FAFSA on the Web at www. fafsa.ed.gov.** Select the "Add or Delete a School Code" link to add school codes to your FAFSA.

2. **If you do not have a PIN, wait until you receive your SAR.** Look for the four-digit Data Release Number (DRN) on the first page of your SAR, and then call 1-800-4-FED-AID (1-800-433-3243) for a customer service representative to add additional school codes to your FAFSA. The DRN, along with your name and Social Security number, verifies your identity.

> 3. The financial aid administrator at a school can add their school code to your FAFSA, if you provide the school with your DRN.
>
> If you need additional help, check with a guidance officer, your local financial aid office, or call 1-800-4-FED-AID and ask to speak with a representative.

Estimated vs. Actual Data

The FAFSA should be completed before your tax returns have been filed, so the information you report may have been estimated. When you have more accurate information or discover that an error was made, update or correct the information. Since most families now file electronically, you can go to the Web site, www.fafsa.ed.gov, and make the necessary changes. If you filled out a paper FAFSA and received a paper SAR in the mail, you can make the changes on the SAR and send it back to the FAFSA processor. Also, every school has the ability to make the corrections to the central processor for you as well.

Additional Document Requirements

When the school receives your output from the CPS, the financial aid office evaluates the information to determine whether additional documents are required. The documents required by each school differ somewhat depending on the types of aid the institution has to offer and whether or not you have been selected for a process called verification.

> Do not get intimidated by financial aid forms. Develop a school deadline spreadsheet and if you need help, ask!

Schools usually assign a deadline for receipt of these additional documents. To avoid jeopardizing the application process, always submit required documents to the institution by their established deadlines. As stated earlier, it is important to submit documents that are complete, signed, and dated so there are no delays in processing or award notification since this can mean significant decreases in aid offered.

CSS/PROFILE®

In addition to the most common aid application, the FAFSA, there is another application called CSS/PROFILE®. This application is sponsored by the College Board and used by about 400 private colleges that devote billions of dollars of their own money to scholarships.

> For a link to the CSS/PROFILE, go to www.collegeboard.com.

PROFILE can only be completed online; there isn't a paper version. If you don't have your own computer, you will have to make arrangements with your school, local library, or someone else to use theirs.

While the FAFSA is free, PROFILE is a fee-based application, costing $25 for the first college and $16 for each additional school. There is an automatic fee waiver built into the application process for families with low income and assets; you do not have to apply for the fee waiver in advance. It is possible, however, that the PROFILE fee will be money well spent since it will give you access to large amounts of college money beyond what the federal and state governments have available.

PROFILE works on an earlier calendar than the FAFSA. While the FAFSA cannot be completed until after the January 1 preceding fall entrance, PROFILE is available as early as the preceding October so it can be used for Early Decision as well as regular admission.

DEADLINES

Nobody likes deadlines and no financial aid administrator finds pleasure in denying a family financial assistance because they failed to meet one. However, deadlines are used because some funds are limited and, for lack of a better way to ration precious resources, schools have resorted to imposing deadlines on financial aid applicants. To ensure the best possible financial aid award, you must meet deadlines.

Since deadlines, especially those in January, are so critical to the successful completion of the application process, let's look at them again, this time by category.

FAFSA

Although the FAFSA indicates a deadline of June 30 of the following year for federal aid, schools usually set much earlier priority filing dates by which you must submit the FAFSA for full consideration for institutional funds. These priority filing dates are typically in the early spring preceding the school year for which you are seeking aid: for example, by February, March, or April for the school year beginning in the fall.

Tax Returns and Institutional Applications

Frequently, schools require copies of tax returns with institutional applications. Deadlines for these documents are usually somewhat later than the application deadline for filing the FAFSA.

Federal Programs

Some federal programs are not dependent upon the availability of funds at a particular school. Funds for these programs are always available, provided that you can demonstrate eligibility. This is not the case with the federal campus-based programs or institutional aid for which funding is quite limited.

HOW "THEY" DECIDE WHAT YOU PAY

At this point, it is important to make a distinction between "need" and "need analysis." Your need, as determined by the school, represents the amount of money needed for your child to attend a particular school. Need analysis, on the other hand, focuses on determining the amount you can reasonably be expected to contribute toward your child's educational expenses for a given year.

Principles of Need Analysis

Since the amount of money available through federal student aid programs is limited, the process of distributing student aid funds must be done in a fair and equitable manner. To understand how need analysis works, it is important to note the basic underlying principles. These are:

> ➤ Parents and students have the primary responsibility to pay for their educational costs to the extent that they are able.

> ➤ Each student's current financial situation should be taken into consideration when determining need.

> ➤ Need analysis must evaluate all student applicants in an equal, fair, and consistent manner.

In general, the need analysis formula considers several factors when determining how much you can reasonably be expected to contribute toward educational expenses. The two most influential factors are:

1. Your income

2. Your asset equity

There are other elements that can affect your ability to pay. These can include:

> ➤ **The number of people in your family**

> ➤ **Family members supported on a fixed income (this influences the amount of discretionary income available for college expenses)**

> ➤ **The number of siblings attending college.** When more than one family member is attending college, the parental portion of the EFC needs to be divided among several individuals instead of just one.

Overview of the Federal Methodology

The Federal Methodology (FM) is the system used to determine the EFC. While there is only one Federal Methodology, there are three computational models contained within the methodology: the regular, simplified, and automatically assessed formulas.

The Regular Formula

The regular need analysis formula is used most. It evaluates your asset situation and determines a contribution from assets, an amount that is combined with available income to give an accurate picture of your financial strength. Here's how it works:

> ➤ **First, your net worth is calculated by adding assets reported on the FAFSA (negative amounts are converted to zero for this calculation).** The formula excludes any part of a family-owned and controlled business with no more than 100 full-time (or equivalent) employees. For all other business, the net worth of a business/farm is adjusted to protect a significant portion of the net worth of these assets.

> ➤ **Second, your discretionary net worth is calculated by subtracting an education savings and asset protection allowance from your net worth.** This is done to protect a portion of assets (net worth). Discretionary net worth may be less than zero.

> ➤ **Finally, the discretionary net worth is multiplied by the conversion rate of 12 percent to obtain your contribution from assets, which represents the portion of the value of your assets that may be considered to be available to help pay your child's college costs.** If the contribution from assets is less than zero, it is set to zero.

Your contribution from assets is added to your available income, and this value is referred to as the adjusted available income. The adjusted available income is multiplied by an assessment rate, which is a percentage that increases as the adjusted available income increases. This finally brings us to the amount in a given year that you are expected to contribute to your child's educational expenses.

If multiple household members attend college at least half-time during the same year, the parental portion of your EFC is divided equally among them. For instance, if your EFC were calculated to be $5,000 and your son and daughter were planning to attend college in the same year, this amount would be shared between the two children. In other words, your family would be expected to provide $2,500 for your son and $2,500 for your daughter (this assumes no student contribution from income or assets).

Simplified Formula or Simplified Needs Test

In some very specific situations, the need analysis formula ignores your asset information. An EFC is computed using only your income; no contribution from assets is assessed. This formula is called the simplified needs test. A dependent student qualifies for the simplified formula if all of the following criteria are met:

> ➤ **The student's parents filed or are eligible to file an IRS form 1040A or 1040EZ, or if they are not required to file any income tax return.**

> ➤ **The student, spouse, or parent(s) is a recipient of a federal means-tested benefit.** This includes Social Security Income (SSI) benefits, food stamps, free or reduced lunches, Temporary Assistance to Needy Families (TANF), or the special supplemental nutrition program for women, infants, and children (WIC). Additional programs may be included by the Secretary of Education.

> ➤ **The income of the parents from the two sources below is $49,999 or less (excluding the student's income).**

> ➤ **For tax filers, the parents' adjusted gross income from form 1040A or 1040EZ is $49,999 or less.**

> ➤ **For non-tax filers, the income shown on the W-2 forms of both parents (plus any other earnings from work not included on the W-2s) is $49,999 or less.**

It is important to emphasize that the key to qualifying for the simplified need formula is not whether you filed a 1040A or 1040EZ but rather whether you were eligible to file one of these types of tax returns. In other words, if your combined income was less than $50,000 and you filed a 1040 but were eligible to file a 1040A or 1040EZ, you would still qualify for the simplified need analysis formula.

Automatically Assessed Formula

This third method of determining an EFC does not involve any calculation. Instead, you are automatically assessed an EFC of zero dollars, which entitles you to the maximum Federal Pell Grant. This model is appropriately termed the Automatic Zero EFC.

Certain students are automatically eligible for a zero EFC. For the award year, a dependent student automatically qualifies for a zero EFC if their parents meet either of the following criteria:

> Some private schools may allow you to reduce your EFC based upon prior payment of elementary or secondary school tuition. Ask the financial aid counselor.

➤ The parents filed or are eligible to file an IRS form 1040A or 1040EZ (they are not required to file a form 1040), or the parents are not required to file any income tax return and the sum of both parents' adjusted gross incomes is $20,000 or less, or if they did not file a tax return, the sum of their earned incomes is $20,000 or less.

➤ The student, spouse, or parent(s) is a recipient of a federal means-tested benefit. This includes Social Security Income (SSI) benefits, food stamps, free or reduced lunches, Temporary Assistance to Needy Families (TANF), or the special supplemental nutrition program for women, infants, and children (WIC). Additional programs may be included by the Secretary of Education.

Special Circumstances

There may be situations in which base-year income does not provide an accurate reflection of your financial strength or other aspects of the formula do not reasonably depict your ability to contribute to educational expenses. Under the Federal Methodology, the aid administrator may change the FM data elements in individual cases in ways that would more accurately measure your ability to pay for educational costs. These professional judgment adjustments may be made only when unusual and extenuating circumstances exist and only when you provide adequate documentation of those circumstances.

A common example of an extenuating circumstance that would lead an aid administrator's use of professional judgment is when you experience a significant loss of income between the base year and the current year. This could happen as a result of a family member losing a job or having hours at work reduced. If this or a similar situation occurs, a financial aid administrator may decide to use your projected or current-year income in the need analysis formula rather than the base year's amount, as long as you provide adequate documentation. You should contact the financial aid office for more information if a significant change in the financial position of your family has changed.

LAST BUT NOT LEAST

By not completing the FAFSA, too many families are "self-determining" that they are ineligible for federal financial aid. According to the American Council on Education, many families whose income is less than $20,000 are not filing a FAFSA. The following chart illustrates the point.

Income	Didn't File a FAFSA
Less than $20,000	20.50%
$20,000–$39,000	31.60%
$40,000–$59,999	43.7%
$60,000–$79,999	46.2%
$80,000 and above	56.9%

Source: American Council on Education

The moral of this story is: Let the financial aid offices determine one's ability to pay. That's what they are trained and paid to do.

Getting Your Share of the Money

FAST FACTS

➤ **Make sure your Federal Pell Grant is listed correctly.** A "0" expected family contribution should give you a maximum Pell Grant of $4,310 per year.

➤ **Many institutions have set aside institutional need-based grant funds that are not advertised.** Go ahead and ask (appeal) for some of those dollars, especially if a school has left you with unmet need.

➤ **If you need to borrow, remember that the terms and conditions of education loans can vary.** Make sure you understand the terms and the costs (i.e., interest rate, loan fees, and repayment schedule) of each loan you are offered.

➤ **Investigate PLUS loans.** If you have sufficient resources to finance your child's college costs but are concerned that you may not have enough cash on hand for all those expenses, the federal government offers a non-need-based loan program—the PLUS loan. All families can take advantage of this program regardless of current income.

The federal government provides more than $90 billion per year in grants, loans, and work programs that provide access to college for millions of eligible students. The trick is knowing how to qualify for them. This chapter describes the individual federal student financial aid programs, with a particular focus on need-based assistance available through the U.S. Department of Education, the U.S. Department of Health and Human Services, and the U.S. Department of the Interior. You will also find out about state, institutional, and private sources of aid.

U.S. DEPARTMENT OF EDUCATION PROGRAMS

The majority of federal student assistance programs were initiated or consolidated by Title IV of the Higher Education Act (HEA) of 1965 and are administered by the U.S. Department of Education. The most common programs are:

- ➤ Federal Pell Grant
- ➤ Federal Supplemental Educational Opportunity Grant (FSEOG)
- ➤ Academic Competitiveness Grants (ACG)
- ➤ National SMART Grants
- ➤ Federal Perkins Loan
- ➤ Federal Work-Study (FWS)
- ➤ Federal Family Education Loan (FFEL) Program
  - Federal Stafford Loan (Subsidized and Unsubsidized)
  - Federal PLUS Loans
- ➤ William D. Ford Federal Direct Loan Program
  - Federal Direct Subsidized and Direct Unsubsidized Loans
  - Federal Direct PLUS Loans

The Federal Pell Grant, FSEOG, ACG, National SMART Grants, Federal Perkins Loan, FWS, Federal Subsidized Stafford, and Direct Subsidized

Loan programs are need-based. Simply stated, this means that when determining eligibility for funds from these programs, your EFC is considered. Federal Unsubsidized Stafford and Direct Unsubsidized Loans, which are discussed in detail later in this chapter, are sometimes referred to as non-need-based programs since your EFC is not considered when determining eligibility for funds from these programs. The William D. Ford Federal Direct Loan Program, commonly referred to as the Direct Loan Program, is a relative newcomer to the financial aid scene. Depending on the program in which the school participates (some schools participate in both), you will borrow from either or both the FFEL Program or Direct Loan Program for a given period of enrollment. Check with your school for more details.

A number of Department of Education funds are allocated through a variety of campus-based programs, including the Federal Supplemental Educational Opportunity Grant (FSEOG) Program, the Federal Work-Study (FWS) Program, and the Federal Perkins Loan Program to participating schools to award to eligible financial aid applicants. Receiving aid from these campus-based programs depends upon the availability of funds at a particular school. This means that school-based awards cannot be transported from one school to another. The types and amount of funds awarded from the campus-based programs may vary from school to school, even if your EFC remains the same and the Cost of Attendance is similar.

A student is eligible for campus-based funds if enrolled full-time, half-time, or even less than half-time, although the amount available to students enrolled less than half-time is generally more limited. Note that campus-based funds are subject to change even after your child begins attending the school, particularly if additional outside funding is received, such as a private scholarship.

The Federal Family Education Loan (FFEL) Program is a set of guaranteed federal student loan programs that include the Federal Subsidized Stafford Loan and Federal Unsubsidized Stafford Loan. These are long-term, low-interest loans available to students attending eligible colleges and universities. Under limited circumstances, these loans may also be used for attendance at eligible international schools. The FFEL Program also includes the PLUS Loan, which is available to parents for paying their children's tuition.

The source of funds for the Federal Family Education Loan Program is private capital from banks, savings and loan associations, credit unions, and other lending institutions. In some cases, schools, state agencies, and private nonprofit agencies may also be lenders. The FFEL Program is administered by guaranty agencies that insure lenders, with the backing of the federal government, against loss if a borrower defaults on the loan or is unable to repay it. You can obtain detailed loan information from your child's school.

General Information and Eligibility Criteria

In addition to demonstrating need, there are other eligibility criteria that must be met to receive money from these federal student assistance programs. Basic eligibility requirements include:

1. **The student must be a U.S. citizen or eligible noncitizen.** U.S. citizen means: citizen of one of the fifty states, the District of Columbia, Puerto Rico, the Virgin Islands, Guam, or the Northern Mariana Islands. An eligible noncitizen includes U.S. nationals; U.S. permanent residents who have an I-151, I-551, or I-551C (Alien Registration Receipt Card); or a person who has an Arrival—Departure Record (I-94) from the BCIS (Bureau of Citizenship and Immigration Services, formerly known as the Immigration and Naturalization Service, or INS) with one of the following designations: Refuge, Asylum Granted, Indefinite Parole, Humanitarian Parole, Cuban-Haitian Entrant, or Conditional Entrant (valid only if issued before April 1, 1980). Note: For the ACG and National SMART Grants, *only* U.S. citizens who are full-time students *and* Pell Grant recipients can be considered.

2. **The student must be enrolled or accepted for enrollment in an eligible degree or certificate program, or other program leading to a recognized education credential, at an eligible postsecondary institution.** Not all postsecondary

schools are approved by the Department of Education to participate in student financial aid programs, either by choice or by exclusion.

In addition, your child must be admitted to the school for the purpose of obtaining a degree, certificate, or other recognized education credential. Students enrolled in a program leading to teacher certification from a state may also receive Federal Pell Grants, FWS, Federal Perkins Loans, and FFEL or Direct Loans.

3. **The student must not be simultaneously enrolled in secondary school.** This criterion has implications for high school students who are completing all or part of their senior year course work at a local college.

4. **The student must have a high school diploma or its recognized equivalent or have the ability to benefit from the course of study.** If your child does not have a high school diploma or its recognized equivalent (usually a General Educational Development certificate or diploma (GED) or a state certificate), he or she must demonstrate the ability to benefit from the training or education. This is accomplished by receiving a passing score on an independently administered test approved by the Department of Education.

If your child excelled academically but did not complete high school and is now seeking enrollment in an educational program leading to at least an associate degree or its equivalent, he or she may, under some circumstances, be eligible for federal assistance. The school's formalized, written policy for admitting such students must be met, and documentation must be provided to the school to show academic excellence in high school.

If your child completed secondary education in a homeschool setting, he or she is eligible for federal aid as long as the homeschool setting is treated as a home school or private school under state law.

5. **The student must provide a valid and verifiable Social Security number.** Through the use of a database match, all

federal financial aid applicants will have their Social Security numbers verified by the Social Security Administration as part of the application process. The student's Social Security number, first and last names, and date of birth are compared with the Social Security Administration's records. Students who fail this match must provide verification of their Social Security number to the school to receive any federal student aid.

If your child uses a name that differs from Social Security records, the Social Security Administration must be notified of a name change well in advance of applying for federal student aid to avoid unnecessary delays and confusion.

6. **The student must sign a Statement of Educational Purpose stating that all federal funds received will be used solely for educational expenses.** All recipients of federal financial aid must sign a statement promising to use any funds received from the federal programs to pay for educational costs at the schools they will attend. Be aware that any federal financial aid money received is to be used to pay for tuition and fees, books and supplies, reasonable living and personal expenses, and other expenses incurred as a direct result of pursuing a postsecondary education. This requirement is satisfied simply by completing and signing the FAFSA, which incorporates the Statement of Educational Purpose in the signature section.

7. **The student must, if required, be registered with the Selective Service.** Upon turning 18, all males must register with the Selective Service. This includes U.S. citizens as well as permanent residents and other eligible noncitizens.

8. **The student must not have had federal benefits suspended or terminated as a result of a drug offense conviction.** Federal student aid eligibility is suspended for any individual convicted of violating any federal or state drug possession or sale law. This applies only if the drug-related offense for which he or she was convicted occurred while the student was receiving federal aid. The date of ineligibility begins on the date of conviction.

9. **The student must maintain satisfactory academic progress in the program of study.** Satisfactory academic progress standards vary from school to school. Generally speaking, to receive federal aid your child must maintain a minimum grade point average and pass a minimum number of credits, units, or clock hours each academic term.

10. **The student must not be in default on a previous federal educational loan, owe an overpayment on a previous federal educational grant or loan, or borrow in excess of federal student loan limits.** If your child is in default or owes an overpayment, eligibility may be regained by paying the debt or making arrangements for payment that are satisfactory to the holder of the debt.

11. **The student must meet additional program-specific criteria.** The following sections describe in detail the student aid programs administered by the U.S. Department of Education. A summary chart of these programs appears on pages 41–45.

Federal Pell Grant Program

The Federal Pell Grant is the second-largest federal student aid program and provides grant assistance to students who have not yet earned a bachelor's or first-professional degree. The intent of the program is to assist the neediest students. Federal Pell Grants may be received while being enrolled full-time, half-time, or even less than half-time. The financial aid administrator calculates the actual award amount based upon your EFC, Cost of Attendance, and enrollment status. Because the Cost of Attendance and enrollment status can vary from school to school, so too can your Federal Pell Grant award.

Some noteworthy characteristics of the Federal Pell Grant:

➢ **It is a grant.** In other words, you don't have to pay it back.

➢ **Eligibility does not depend on the availability of funds at a particular school.** Rather, if you apply by the federal application deadline, demonstrate a required level of need, and meet all of the general and program eligibility criteria, you will receive some amount of support from the Federal Pell Grant Program.

> **It is portable.** If you are eligible for a Federal Pell Grant, you may use it for study at any eligible school in any eligible program.

> **The annual amount of your Federal Pell Grant depends, in part, on the amount that Congress appropriates for the program.** For 2008–09, the maximum award amount based on congressional appropriations is $4,310. The minimum amount is $400.

Federal Supplemental Educational Opportunity Grant (FSEOG) Program

The FSEOG Program provides grant funds for exceptionally needy undergraduate students who have not yet earned a bachelor's or first-professional degree. Priority is given to students who are eligible for a Federal Pell Grant and who have the lowest EFC as determined by the school. The minimum annual FSEOG award that may be received from a school is $100 and the maximum is $4,000.

The minimum award may be prorated if your child is enrolled for less than a full academic year; if enrolled in approved study-abroad programs, your child can receive up to $4,400 a year. Like the Federal Pell Grant, FSEOG is gift aid, meaning that it does not have to be earned or repaid. However, unlike Federal Pell Grants, the actual amount awarded is subject to the availability of funds at the school your child chooses to attend.

Academic Competitiveness Grants (ACG)

Academic Competitiveness Grants provide need-based grants for U.S. citizens who are Federal Pell Grant recipients and who are enrolled full-time as a first or second year student in a qualifying program of study. ACG require the completion of a rigorous secondary school program, as determined by the U.S. Department of Education and the Higher Education authority in the state the college or university is located. There are a number of options for determining eligibility for this program, and they may vary from state to state. In general, a student should have completed 4 years of English, 3 years of math, 3 years of science, 3 years of social studies, and 1 year of a foreign language. Students can also be determined eligible if they demonstrate that they have taken two Advanced Placement (AP) or International Baccalaureate (IB) courses and received a score of 3 or higher on the AP exams and a 4 or higher on the IB exams. This program is open to home-schooled students and transfer students. Grants are for up to $750 in the first year and up to $1,300 in the second year. Students must maintain a 3.0 GPA.

National Science and Mathematics Access to Retain Talent (SMART) Grant

National SMART Grants provide need-based grants to U.S. citizens who are Federal Pell Grant recipients and are in the third or fourth year of a baccalaureate degree program. Students must be enrolled full-time in an eligible major with a cumulative GPA of 3.0 on a 4.0 scale. Majors include computer science, engineering, certain foreign languages, life sciences, mathematics, physical sciences, technology, and multidisciplinary studies. Students should check with the financial aid office for more specific information on approved majors. National SMART grants are for up to $4,000 per year and cannot exceed the COA.

Federal Perkins Loan Program

The Federal Perkins Loan Program, the oldest loan program administered by the Department of Education, is a source of low-interest loans (currently 5 percent) for undergraduate, graduate, and professional students. No interest is charged as long as your child is enrolled in school at least half-time. Schools are required to give priority to students with exceptional financial need when awarding Federal Perkins Loans. Undergraduate students can borrow as much as $4,000 each year and up to an aggregate maximum of $20,000 for undergraduate study.

Students who participate in an approved study-abroad program can also receive a Federal Perkins Loan. In fact, your child may be eligible to borrow annual and aggregate loan maximums that exceed the amounts noted previously by as much as 20 percent.

Repayment of a Federal Perkins Loan begins either nine months after either graduation or after a student ceases to be enrolled at least half-time. This is called a grace period. Depending upon the amount borrowed, the maximum repayment period may be as long as ten years. Borrowers who qualify because of low income may be granted an additional ten years to repay their loan. There is no penalty for prepaying all or part of a Federal Perkins Loan.

In addition to meeting the general eligibility criteria, Federal Perkins Loan borrowers must:

➢ Receive a determination of eligibility or ineligibility for a Federal Pell Grant

➢ Be willing and able to repay the loan

➢ Provide a driver's license number (if your child has one)

Repayment can be postponed or interrupted for specified periods of time if certain conditions are met. The postponement of repayment is commonly referred to as a deferment. All loans are deferred while your child is enrolled at least half-time at an eligible school. Some deferments carry very specific conditions, and some have limits on their length. Interest does not accrue during periods of deferment, and after each deferment period your child is entitled to another six-month grace period before repayment resumes. In addition, periods of deferment do not count toward the normal ten-year maximum for repayment. Under other, more limited, conditions, your child may be eligible to have all or part of his or her Perkins Loan forgiven, which means he or she doesn't have to repay part (or sometimes all) of the loan. See your financial aid administrator for more details on deferments and forgiveness of these loans.

Federal Work-Study (FWS) Program

The Federal Work-Study Program provides jobs for students who need earnings to meet a portion of their education expenses. Both undergraduate and graduate students are eligible to receive FWS assistance. The federal government provides funds that pay up to 75 percent of the wages, and the school or other employer pays the rest. In addition, if the school your child plans to attend participates in the America Reads or America Counts initiatives, up to 100 percent of the FWS wages may be provided for those programs. Contact the school for more information.

The number of hours that a student must work each week varies from school to school and from student to student. This is related to the amount of the work-study award, the hourly pay rate, or the amount of time the student is available to work.

Unlike the other federal student aid programs, there are no limits on the amount that the school may award in Federal Work-Study as long as the amount awarded and other resources do not exceed a student's need. To ensure that the number of hours worked is not so great as to interfere with your child's academic studies, schools usually have a policy regarding reasonable work-study award amounts. Although students normally earn their FWS awards by working during the academic year, some schools allow part or all of the awards to be earned during the summer or school breaks.

> Federal Work-Study funds are not considered income for the next year's FAFSA.

Employment can be on campus or off campus. An employer can be the school itself, the state, a local public or federal agency (except the Department of Education), or a private nonprofit or for-profit organization. Federal Work-Study employees must be paid an amount that is at least equal to the current federal minimum wage. The type of work performed as a work-study student varies. Food service worker and clerical assistant positions are fairly common, especially for students with no prior work experience. Lab assistants, library aides, and other more specialized positions are also usually available. Some schools place FWS recipients in specific jobs, while others simply post FWS openings and allow the placement process to be competitive.

If your child receives an FWS award, you should be aware of the following:

> ➤ FWS awards must be earned, and payment is based on the number of hours actually worked.

> You must communicate with the financial aid office or the student employment office to obtain a work-study position.

Federal Stafford Loans

The Federal Stafford Loan Program is the largest source of low-interest loans to students administered by the U.S. Department of Education. Federal Stafford Loans are available to both undergraduate and graduate students. Many schools automatically include a Federal Stafford Loan as part of their financial aid package and notify you of exactly how much may be borrowed from that program. Be mindful that, unlike the Federal Pell Grant and campus-based programs, to receive a Federal Stafford Loan an additional loan application may need to be completed (in addition to the FAFSA). Check with your child's school to find out if he or she needs to complete this application. If a Federal Stafford Loan is offered, the school usually sends information about the application process along with the official notification of financial assistance. You can also obtain Federal Stafford Loan applications from participating lenders. Most families now apply for these loans electronically. The financial aid office will help guide you through this process. Loans for subsequent years are easily done with your lender on the Web.

To ensure that your child is familiar with the terms and responsibilities of borrowing and that he or she fully understands that the loan must be repaid, your child is required to have loan counseling before receiving any Federal Stafford Loan funds. Once the loan counseling requirement is satisfied, the school either uses the loan funds to offset charges for tuition, fees, and room and board or will give the loan proceeds directly to your child. The funds may be used to buy books or pay for other costs incidental to attending the school.

Loans made under this program can be subsidized, unsubsidized, or a combination of both. Because the concepts of subsidized and unsubsidized loans may be new to you, let's look at them in more detail.

Federal Subsidized Stafford Loans (need-based)

A subsidized loan means that the federal government pays the interest to the lender while a student is in school and during other periods when the student is not required to make payments. Because the government is paying the interest during periods of enrollment, the student is not responsible for paying the interest and interest does not accrue until repayment begins. Once in repayment, the student is then responsible for paying the interest on the loan as well as the principal amount borrowed. There is a fixed interest rate on all Stafford Loans.

To receive a Federal Subsidized Stafford Loan, need must be demonstrated under the federal need formula. In other words, when your EFC is subtracted from the Cost of Attendance, the result must be greater than zero for you to be eligible to borrow a Federal Subsidized Stafford Loan. Borrowing is further limited by other aid your child has been awarded, as well as the annual maximum loan limits applicable to the program.

Unsubsidized Federal Stafford Loans (non-need-based)

Unsubsidized loans provide assistance to students who may not demonstrate need according to the need formula discussed earlier but who would benefit from having access to a low-interest federal student loan program. An unsubsidized loan means that the federal government does not pay the interest on your child's behalf. Instead, all of the interest that accrues is paid throughout the life of the loan, including interest that accrues while your child is enrolled in school. There is a fixed interest rate on all Stafford Loans.

Interest that accrues while your child is enrolled in school can be paid in one of two ways:

1. Pay the interest as it accrues.

2. Have the interest capitalized (interest is added to the loan principal and must be repaid when your child leaves school).

Another major difference with an unsubsidized loan is that the EFC is not considered when determining eligibility. This is why unsubsidized loans are often referred to as non-need-based. Eligibility for an unsubsidized loan is determined using an alternate need formula, which requires the school to subtract any estimated financial assistance, including any Federal Subsidized Stafford Loan eligibility, from the Cost of Attendance. The result of this equation is the maximum amount that you may borrow from the Federal Unsubsidized Stafford Loan Program. However, in no case may the amount borrowed exceed the annual loan maximums discussed later in this section.

This difference in the definition of need means that unlike the Federal Subsidized Stafford Loan, a Federal Unsubsidized Stafford Loan may be used to replace the EFC, provided it has not already been replaced by some other form of aid.

Many students are eligible to borrow a combination of Federal Subsidized and Unsubsidized Stafford Loans. Eligibility for a Federal Subsidized Stafford Loan must always be determined before securing a Federal Unsubsidized Stafford Loan to ensure that the least costly, and thus most desirable, loans are secured first. If eligibility for a Federal Unsubsidized Stafford Loan remains, you may borrow that as well, as long as annual loan limits are not exceeded.

In addition to the general eligibility requirements listed earlier, to be eligible to receive a Federal Stafford Loan your child must:

➤ Be enrolled or accepted for enrollment on at least a half-time basis.

➤ Obtain a determination of eligibility or ineligibility for a Federal Pell Grant.

➤ Be enrolled in a school with an acceptable loan default rate among its previous borrowers.

Stafford Loan Limits

The total combined amounts that may be borrowed in Subsidized and Unsubsidized Stafford Loans may not exceed the annual loan limits, which are specified in law and regulation. The maximum amounts that may be borrowed are:

➤ $3,500 per year for first-year undergraduate students

➤ $4,500 per year for second-year undergraduate students

➤ $5,500 per year for the remaining years of undergraduate study

All students are limited in the total amount they can borrow from the Federal Stafford Loan Program during their undergraduate and graduate academic careers. These borrowing limits are referred to as aggregate loan maximums and will vary depending on whether your child is an undergraduate or graduate student.

Dependent undergraduate students may borrow $23,000 in Subsidized and Unsubsidized loans. Dependent or independent undergraduate students whose parents do not qualify for PLUS Loans may borrow $23,000 from the Federal Subsidized Stafford Program and $46,000 from the Federal Unsubsidized Stafford Loan Program, less any amounts borrowed from the Federal Subsidized Stafford Loan Program.

The interest rate charged on Federal Subsidized and Unsubsidized Stafford Loans is fixed. The same terms and conditions apply to Federal Unsubsidized Stafford Loans, except that your child is responsible for the interest while enrolled in college and during the repayment period.

Lenders were authorized to charge origination fees of 2 percent of the principal amount of the loan for 2006–07. This fee is being reduced by 0.5 percent per year until it is eliminated as of July 1, 2010. In addition, there is a default fee of 1 percent of the principal amount of the loan. These fees may be deducted from loan proceeds by the lender. Check with your lender.

In addition to the Federal Stafford Loan limits just listed, dependent students whose parents applied for and were not able to get a PLUS Loan may borrow up to:

➤ $7,500 per year for first-year students enrolled in a program of study that is at least a full academic year (at least $4,000 of this must be in Unsubsidized loans)

➤ $8,500 per year for students who have completed the first year of academic study and the remainder of their program is at least a full academic year (at least $4,000 of this must be in Unsubsidized loans)

> $10,500 per year for students who have completed two years of academic study and the remainder of their program is at least a full academic year (at least $5,000 of this must be in Unsubsidized loans)

Payment of loan principal and, in the case of Subsidized loans, interest does not begin until six months after your child graduates or ceases to be enrolled at least half-time. The loans must be repaid within ten years of the date repayment begins, excluding periods of deferment and forbearance. For students with higher balances, the repayment period can be extended.

Deferments and Cancellations

Deferments allow borrowers who meet certain criteria to postpone or interrupt repayment. The deferments available to Federal Stafford Loans are similar to those found in the Federal Perkins Loan Program but, unlike in the Federal Perkins Loan Program, there is only one grace period. See your financial aid administrator or lender for more information about deferments.

Cancellation of a Federal Stafford Loan is available in the event of your child's death or permanent and total disability. In addition, a portion of the loan may be repaid by your child's participation in some national and community service programs. Ask your financial aid administrator or lender for more details on loan cancellation and forgiveness options.

In addition, the Department of Education offers loan cancellation options for eligible teachers, including:

> Up to $5,000 of Stafford Loans for a teacher who is teaching full-time in a qualifying low-income elementary or secondary school and began his or her teaching service on or after October 30, 2004. The teacher must be "highly qualified."

> Up to $17,500 of Stafford Loans for a teacher who is teaching in a qualifying low-income secondary school and began his or her teaching service on or after October 30, 2004. The teacher must be "highly qualified" in math or science.

> Up to $17,500 of Stafford Loans for a teacher who is teaching full time in a qualifying low-income elementary or secondary school

and began his or her teaching service on or after October 30, 2004. The teacher must be "highly qualified" in special education.

➤ Up to 100 percent of Perkins Loans for a teacher who received his or her loan after July 1, 1987, and who meets any of the following requirements:

- Teaches in a school that serves low-income students

- Teaches in a school system that has a shortage of teachers in a designated subject

- Teaches disabled students in a public or other nonprofit elementary or secondary school

Perkins Loans are canceled based on the following years of teaching service:

➤ 15 percent canceled per year for each of the first and second years

➤ 20 percent canceled per year for each of the third and fourth years

➤ 30 percent canceled for the fifth year

Forgiveness is also available to teachers who began their teaching service before October 30, 2004, and meet certain criteria.

Federal PLUS Loans

Federal PLUS Loans are for parents of dependent students and are designed to help families with cash-flow problems. There is no needs test to qualify, and the loans are made by FFEL lenders. The loan has a fixed interest rate of 8.5 percent, and there is no specific yearly limit; parents can borrow up to the cost of their child's education, less other financial aid received. Repayment begins 60 days after the money is advanced. There is an origination fee of 3 percent of the principal amount of the loan. In addition, there is a default fee of 1 percent of the principal amount of the loan. These fees may be deducted from the loan proceeds by the lender. Check with your lender for details. Parent borrowers must generally have a good credit record to qualify for PLUS Loans.

Deferments allow parent borrowers who meet certain criteria to postpone or interrupt repayment. Contact your loan holder for information regarding deferment eligibility. Cancellation of a Federal PLUS Loan is available in the event of your death or permanent and total disability or your child's death.

William D. Ford Federal Direct Loan Program

The federal government launched the William D. Ford Federal Direct Loan Program in 1994. This program includes Direct Subsidized and Direct Unsubsidized Loans. You may also hear the various programs referred to as the Direct Subsidized Stafford Loan or the Direct Unsubsidized Stafford Loan. The terms and conditions of loans made under the Direct Loan Program are nearly identical to those made under the FFEL Program except for the source of loan funds, some aspects of the application process, and the administrative details of the repayment process. Most schools participate in one program or the other.

Federal Direct Subsidized and Direct Unsubsidized Loan Program

Just as the Federal Stafford Loan program offers both subsidized and unsubsidized student loans, so does the Direct Loan Program. Technically, Direct Subsidized and Direct Unsubsidized Loans are exactly the same as Federal Subsidized and Unsubsidized Stafford Loans. For instance, to receive a Direct Subsidized or Direct Unsubsidized Loan, you must complete and submit a FAFSA, and first-time loan recipients are also required to attend a loan counseling session prior to receiving payment.

Federal Direct PLUS Loan Program

Just as the FFEL Program offers a Federal PLUS Loan for parents, so does the Direct Loan Program. The terms and conditions of a Direct PLUS Loan are generally the same as a Federal PLUS loan, with the interest rate and some repayment plan options being exceptions.

Summary Information on Undergraduate Student Aid Programs Administered by the U.S. Department of Education

Program	Description	Annual/ Aggregate	Eligibility	Repayment Required
Federal Pell Grant	Grant program	Annual minimum and maximum vary; for 2008–09, maximum $4,310; no aggregate	Students without baccalaureate or first-professional degree	No
Federal Supplemental Educational Opportunity Grant (FSEOG)	Campus-based grant program; funds awarded by institution	$100 annual minimum; $4,000 annual maximum; no aggregate (students in approved study-abroad programs may receive up to $4,400)	Students without baccalaureate or first-professional degree; first to students with exceptional financial need; priority to Federal Pell Grant recipients	No
Academic Competitiveness Grants	Grant program	$750 1st year; $1,300 2nd academic year	U.S. citizens only; full-time (12 cr.); Pell Grant eligible; completed rigorous high school curriculum; financial need; 3.0 GPA required	No
National SMART Grants	Grant program	Up to $4,000 for 3rd and 4th academic years	U.S. citizens only; full-time (12 cr.); Pell Grant eligible; enrolled in selected majors; financial need; 3.0 GPA required	No

Summary Information on Undergraduate Student Aid Programs Administered by the U.S. Department of Education *(continued)*

Program	Description	Annual/ Aggregate	Eligibility	Repayment Required
Federal Work-Study (FWS)	Campus-based employment program; funds awarded by institution	N/A	Undergraduate students	No
Federal Perkins Loan	Campus-based loan program; funds awarded by institution	$4,000/year for a maximum of $20,000; funds awarded by institution; interest; study-abroad students may be eligible to borrow annual and aggregate loan maximums that exceed the above-noted amounts by as much as 20 percent	First to students with exceptional financial need; must have determination of eligibility/ ineligibility for Federal Pell Grant	Yes; begins 9 months after cessation of at least half-time enrollment; deferment possible; cancellation provisions
Federal Stafford Loan (Subsidized and Unsubsidized)	Federal Family Education Loan; funds from private capital; interest rate of 6.8 percent (6 percent as of July 1, 2008)	$3,500/1st year; $4,500/ 2nd year; $5,500/each remaining year at undergraduate level; annual maximums prorated for programs and remaining periods of enrollment; undergraduate maximum is $23,000	Students enrolled at least half-time; must have determination of eligibility for Federal Subsidized Stafford before applying for Federal Unsubsidized Stafford	Yes; begins 6 months after cessation of at least half-time enrollment; deferment possible; no interest subsidy on Unsubsidized loan; cancellation provisions

Summary Information on Undergraduate Student Aid Programs Administered by the U.S. Department of Education *(continued)*

Program	Description	Annual/ Aggregate	Eligibility	Repayment Required
Additional Unsubsidized Federal Stafford Loan (additional eligibility for independent undergraduates and certain dependent undergraduates)	Federal Family Education Loan; funds from private capital; interest rate of 6.8 percent	$7,500 1st year; $8,500 2nd year; $10,500/each remaining year at undergraduate level; annual maximums prorated for programs or remaining periods of enrollment; undergraduate maximum, $46,000 undergraduate aggregate, less amounts borrowed in Subsidized Stafford	Independent students and dependent students whose parents are ineligible for a Federal PLUS; must have determination of eligibility for Federal Subsidized Stafford before applying for Federal Unsubsidized Stafford	Yes; begins 6 months after cessation of at least half-time enrollment; deferment possible; no interest subsidy on Unsubsidized loan; cancellation provisions
Federal PLUS Loan	Federal Family Education Loan; funds from private capital; interest rate of 8.5 percent	No annual or aggregate amounts, except parents may not borrow more than the difference between Cost of Attendance and estimated financial assistance	Parents of eligible dependent undergraduates who are enrolled at least half-time; no adverse credit history	Yes; begins 60 days after final disbursement; deferment possible; cancellation provisions

Summary Information on Undergraduate Student Aid Programs Administered by the U.S. Department of Education *(continued)*

Program	Description	Annual/ Aggregate	Eligibility	Repayment Required
Direct Subsidized/ Direct Unsubsidized Loan	William D. Ford Federal Direct Loan; funds awarded by the institution at participating schools; interest rate of 6.8 percent (6 percent as of July 1, 2008)	$3,500 1st year; $4,500 2nd year; $5,500 each remaining year at undergraduate level; annual maximums prorated for programs or remaining periods of enrollment; total undergraduate maximum, $23,000	Undergraduate students; enrolled at least half-time; must have determination of eligibility for Federal Pell Grant; must determine eligibility for Direct Subsidized Loan before applying for Direct Unsubsidized Loan; must attend a participating school	Yes; begins 6 months after cessation of at least half-time enrollment; deferments possible; no interest subsidy on Unsubsidized loan; cancellation provisions
Additional Direct Unsubsidized Loan (additional eligibility for independent undergraduates and certain dependent undergraduates)	William D. Ford Federal Direct Loan; funds awarded by the institution at participating schools; interest rate of 6.8 percent	$7,500 1st year; $8,500 2nd year; $10,500 each remaining year at undergraduate level; annual maximums prorated for programs or remaining periods of enrollment; total undergraduate maximum, $46,000, less amounts borrowed in Subsidized Direct Loan	Independent students and dependent students whose parents are unable to secure a PLUS Loan; must attend a participating school	Yes; begins 6 months after cessation of at least half-time enrollment; deferments possible; no interest subsidy on Unsubsidized loan; cancellation provisions

Summary Information on Undergraduate Student Aid Programs Administered by the U.S. Department of Education *(continued)*

Program	*Description*	*Annual/ Aggregate*	*Eligibility*	*Repayment Required*
Direct PLUS Loan	William D. Ford Federal Direct Loan; funds awarded by the institution at participating schools; interest rate of 7.9 percent	No annual or aggregate amounts, except borrower cannot borrow more than the difference between Cost of Attendance and estimated financial assistance	Parents of eligible dependent undergraduates who are enrolled at least half-time; no adverse credit history; student must attend a participating school	Yes; begins 60 days after final disbursement; deferment possible; cancellation provisions

U.S. DEPARTMENT OF HEALTH AND HUMAN SERVICES PROGRAMS

In addition to the student aid programs administered by the U.S. Department of Education, several student aid programs are administered by the Department of Health and Human Services (HHS) for the health and nursing professions:

➤ Nursing Student Loan

➤ Health Professions Student Loan

➤ Scholarships for Disadvantaged Students

➤ National Health Service Corps Scholarships

With the exception of the National Health Service Corps Scholarships, the above programs are similar to the Department of Education's campus-based programs: monies are allocated to the schools to distribute to their eligible students in designated health-care fields. Schools are responsible for managing and awarding program funds according to requirements specified by the Department of Health and Human Services.

Nursing Student Loan

The Nursing Student Loan (NSL) Program provides low-interest loans to nursing students attending approved nursing schools. Approved schools must offer:

- ➤ Diploma
- ➤ Associate degree
- ➤ Baccalaureate or equivalent degree
- ➤ Graduate degree in nursing

Loans may be made for full-time or half-time enrollment, and recipients must be citizens, U.S. nationals, or permanent residents. Schools themselves determine application and selection procedures. In most cases, nursing students who complete the FAFSA and any other required application materials are automatically considered for this program provided that they have need.

Schools may award up to $2,500 per academic year depending upon need. This annual limit increases to $4,000 during the final two years of a nursing program. The aggregate NSL maximum is $13,000. The interest rate on the NSL is 5 percent, and repayment of principal and interest begins nine months after your child graduates or ceases to be enrolled at least half-time. Payments may be made on a monthly or quarterly basis. Borrowers have up to ten years to repay their NSL.

Health Professions Student Loan

The Health Professions Student Loan (HPSL) Program provides financial assistance to students enrolled in specific health professions fields. Assistance is provided in the form of long-term, low-interest loans. HPSL interest rates are fixed at 5 percent throughout the life of the loan. Loans may be made to full-time students pursuing a course of study leading to a bachelor or doctor of science degree in pharmacy or a doctor of dentistry, podiatric medicine, optometry, or veterinary medicine degree.

Schools must use parental information when determining a student's eligibility for the HPSL, even if the student is considered independent. The annual maximum that can be borrowed is equal to tuition plus $2,500. There is no aggregate maximum. Repayment of principal and interest begins one year after your child ceases full-time study. The loans must be paid within ten years in equal or graduated installments.

Scholarships for Disadvantaged Students

The Scholarships for Disadvantaged Students (SDS) program was developed to assist students from disadvantaged backgrounds who have demonstrated a commitment to pursuing a career in the health professions. Participating schools are allocated funds on an annual basis.

SDS funds may be used to pay for tuition and other reasonable educational expenses and reasonable living expenses incurred while enrolled as a full-time student. The amount of the scholarship may not exceed the total amount of these required expenses for a specific year.

National Health Service Corps Scholarships

This program is designed to attract health professionals to the National Health Service Corps (NHSC) to practice in areas where there is a shortage of primary-care medical professionals. Students who pursue full-time courses of study in the following fields are eligible to apply:

- ➢ Allopathic or osteopathic medical school
- ➢ Family nurse practitioner program (master's degree in nursing, post-master's or post-baccalaureate certificate)
- ➢ Nurse-midwifery program (master's degree in nursing, post-master's or post-baccalaureate certificate)
- ➢ Physician assistant program (certificate, associate, baccalaureate, or master's program)
- ➢ Dental school

Scholars attending medical school are expected to complete residency programs in one of the following specialties:

> Family medicine

> General pediatrics

> General internal medicine

> Obstetrics/gynecology

> Psychiatry

> Rotating internship (D.O.s only) with a request to complete one of the above specialties

Dental Scholars may do residencies in general practice or pediatric dentistry. The scholarship covers tuition and required fees and provides a stipend for twelve months. NHSC recipients incur a service requirement of one year for each year the scholarship is received, with a minimum of two years service required.

U.S. DEPARTMENT OF THE INTERIOR: BUREAU OF INDIAN AFFAIRS GRANTS

The U.S. Department of the Interior provides grants under the auspices of the Bureau of Indian Affairs (BIA). This agency administers a higher education grant program for enrolled members of an Indian, Eskimo, or Aleut tribe who are pursuing an undergraduate or graduate degree at an accredited postsecondary institution. In order to be eligible for a Bureau of Indian Affairs Grant, students must show financial need as determined by the school they are attending. Additional information may be obtained from any Bureau of Indian Affairs Office.

ALTERNATIVE LOAN PROGRAMS

Once your financial aid awards have been totaled and subtracted from your total COA, there may still be a gap. Private loans, also known as alternative loans, allow you to borrow money to cover this gap. An alternative loan is an education loan that is made by a private lender to the student borrower, and the loan is not guaranteed by either the federal or state government. Although the interest rate for alternative loans may be slightly higher than the interest rate for Perkins or Stafford Loans, alternative loans can still provide the additional funding necessary for college education expenses. When you begin to explore alternative loans, shop around and find the features that are most beneficial to you.

Features of Alternative Loans

Most alternative loans require certification by a financial aid officer at your school, and the maximum you can borrow is the total cost of education minus any other financial aid. Sounds like the PLUS Loan maximum amount, doesn't it? So, can families or students get both? Yes, but the total amount of the student's alternative loan and the parent's loan cannot exceed the student's total COA minus any other financial aid. As far as how much the actual disbursement will be, subtract any fees that may be

> Although each individual lender sets the repayment terms, many alternative loans offer zero payments while the student is in school.

charged by the individual lender from the loan amount. Look for zero-fee loans when shopping for alternative loans. Once again, the school's financial aid office is the place to begin researching alternative loans. Ask for their list of alternative loan lenders and begin comparing the lenders' fees, interest rates, and repayment terms.

The interest rates for alternative loans vary, and many are tied to the prime rate. Prime rate is a term used to describe the interest rate that banks charge to their most creditworthy customers. Alternative loan lenders may advertise "Prime plus 1 percent" or "Prime plus zero percent," which means that your interest rate is variable, depending upon the fluctuations of the prime rate. The interest rate, amount borrowed, and repayment period are all components of the monthly repayment amount.

STATE NEED-BASED AID

Most state student financial assistance programs are need-based and restricted to residents of that state and/or attendance at a school in that state. Over the past few years, there has been a marked increase in state-sponsored merit scholarship programs that are not need-based. Some states have reciprocity agreements that allow students to use their state grants and scholarships to attend schools in any state included in the agreement. In some cases, state aid takes the form of financial support of the school, or grants are made directly to the school but not on behalf of any particular student.

The conditions for need-based student aid vary by state as does the type and form of aid offered. A state may offer scholarships, grants, loans, and/or work programs with their own unique eligibility requirements. Contact appropriate state agencies for updated information on their programs, including amounts of aid, eligibility requirements, and application procedures and deadlines.

Leveraging Educational Assistance Partnership (LEAP) Program

Under the LEAP Program, federal funds are allocated to states to encourage the establishment and expansion of state scholarship and grant assistance to postsecondary students. The federal allotment must be matched by funds appropriated by the state.

Specific eligibility requirements for LEAP funds are determined at the state level. Federal regulations authorize state agencies to extend eligibility to undergraduates and, if desired, to graduate students and less-than-half-time students. However, recipients must meet federal student aid eligibility requirements and demonstrate substantial financial need as determined by the state.

Students apply to their state agency either directly or through the school. The maximum annual LEAP award is $5,000. State agencies have the option of setting lower maximum award amounts. States that allocate their own funds to the program may offer a higher annual maximum award.

INSTITUTIONAL AND PRIVATE SOURCES OF NEED-BASED AID

Many schools have their own resources that are earmarked for student aid. This aid may be merit- or need-based or a combination of the two and may take the form of grants, loans, or employment. Schools often receive contributions from private or corporate donors with specific restrictions attached to the use of those funds. There may be a large variety of small programs with variable requirements or a large pot of discretionary funds for the aid administrator or other school staff or faculty members to award. Discretionary funds might have strict need requirements or might be set aside to help address emergency situations unanticipated when the student's aid was originally awarded. At some schools, institutional aid might be awarded on the same basis as federal campus-based aid. In any case, you should not overlook this source of funding from the school or from individual academic departments within the school.

REPAYING STUDENT LOANS

If it is determined that a student loan is necessary to fund your child's education, there are some important things you need to know about repayment. Here are some commonly asked questions about repaying student loans and answers that will give you the tips you need when it comes time for your child to repay his or her student loan:

> **What is a grace period?** A grace period is allotted to loan borrowers, during which time they do not need to begin repaying their loan. In the case of a Stafford Loan, the grace period is six months after a student finishes school or drops below half-time enrollment. However, prepayments can be made during the grace period. If the loan is subsidized, those payments will be applied directly to the principal of the loan, allowing the loan to be paid off sooner than expected.

> **Is a student loan legally binding?** A Master Promissory Note (MPN) must be signed in order to borrow money for financing higher education. This legally binding document obligates your

child to repay the loan as stated in the terms and conditions of the MPN.

➢ **Are there benefits to repayment?** In addition to earning a good credit rating that will provide lifelong benefits to your child, there are also interest rate reductions for consecutive, on-time payments.

➢ **What if my child decides to go on to graduate school?** Should your child decide to go on to graduate school, any student loan financing used to fund undergraduate schooling will be deferred until graduation from grad school.

➢ **What are the payment methods for making student loan payments?** There are several options in making payments on student loans. In most cases, your child will be offered the opportunity to make payments online, mail in checks, or participate in an automatic debit program in which payments are withdrawn from a designated bank account on a monthly basis. Enrolling in an automatic debit program may result in an interest rate reduction.

➢ **What if my child is having a hard time making loan payments?** There are several repayment scheduling options available:

- **Standard Repayment Schedule:** Payments are the same each month but may be adjusted each year to reflect the variable interest rate. Total repayment schedule is ten years.

- **Graduated Repayment Schedule:** Smaller monthly payments are made early in the repayment schedule and larger payments later in the schedule. Total repayment schedule is ten years.

- **Income-Sensitive/Contingent Repayment Schedule:** Loan payments are based on monthly income. Total repayment term may be extended beyond ten years.

- **Extended Repayment Schedule:** If certain eligibility criteria are met, the repayment term may be extended up to twenty-five years. Loans may be repaid under a standard or graduated repayment schedule.

➢ **What if my child misses a payment?** One missed payment will not place your child's loan into default. However, it will appear on his or her credit record and may affect his or her ability to obtain additional credit. If it is not possible to make a payment, your child should contact the servicer of the loan and explain the situation. In some cases, your child may be eligible for a deferment or forbearance. The worst thing the borrower can do is miss the payment without contacting the loan's holder or become habitually late in making payments.

➤ **What is a student loan deferment?** Deferment is an authorized temporary suspension of repayment. This may be granted under certain circumstances that must be discussed with the holder of the loan. A deferment is not automatic; borrowers must apply, meet certain qualifications, and make arrangements with the holder of the loan. Until notified regarding eligibility for deferment, borrowers should continue making up-to-date payments. Your child is not responsible for paying the interest that accrues during a deferment period on subsidized loans.

➤ **What is forbearance?** A student loan forbearance allows the borrower to reduce the amount of his or her student loan payment or temporarily stop making payments. However, interest continues to accrue during a forbearance period. If your child is financially unable to make payments under the terms of the repayment schedule, a request of forbearance can be made for:

- A short period during which no payment is made

- An extension of time for making payments

- A period in which smaller payments than were originally scheduled are made

➤ **Can anyone get forbearance?** Unlike a student loan deferment, forbearance is granted at the discretion of the lender of the loan. However, the loan holder must grant forbearance upon receipt of the reason for the request and proper documentation if:

- The borrower is a dental or medical intern.

- The monthly student loan payments equal or exceed 20 percent of the borrower's monthly income.

- The borrower is serving in a national service position.

- The borrower qualifies under the Student Loan Repayment Program administered by the U.S. Department of Defense.

- The borrower is affected by a local or national emergency.

- The borrower is a member of the National Guard or Reserves and is mobilized.

- The borrower resides in a designated disaster area.

➢ **What are the consequences if my child does not repay a loan?** The consequences for nonrepayment are very serious, having a long-term effect on your child's life. They include:

- Your child may not be able to obtain more credit, for example, to buy a car or house.

- Your child may be turned down for a credit card.

- Your child could forfeit his or her tax refunds.

- Your child's employer can be ordered to withhold what he or she owes from his or her paycheck.

- Your child may be sued, owe collection and attorney fees, and still be responsible for repaying the loan.

➢ **Is loan consolidation a good idea if my child has to take out more than one loan?** It may be easier to repay several loans at one time by consolidating them into one monthly payment that can be extended up to thirty years. Although the monthly payment can be lower, borrowers may pay a larger amount of total interest. In some cases, the interest rate on a consolidation loan may be higher than the rates on the original loans. Before consolidating loans, contact the loan representative to make sure that loan consolidation would be in your child's best interest. It is important to shop around for the best offer. Read all of the details carefully; you don't want to end up paying more or for a longer period of time than necessary.

➢ **When should borrowers contact their loan holder?** During school, borrowers should contact their loan holder if there are any changes in name, address, telephone number, or enrollment status. Afterward, borrowers are required to inform the holder when they graduate, leave school, or drop below half-time enrollment status. During repayment, borrowers should inform the loan holder of a change in name, address, or telephone number. It is important to notify the holder if the payments cannot be made or if payments will be late.

Your child should have no problem meeting the responsibilities of student loan repayment if he or she sticks to a realistic budget and works with the loan holder to create a payment schedule that works. The best repayment strategy is to schedule monthly payments as high as his or her budget will allow, without endangering the possibility of making those payments.

Although a student loan is ultimately your child's responsibility, it often falls to the parent to reiterate the importance of that commitment while planning for college.

MORE RESOURCES

FAFSA on the Web is the clearinghouse for federal financial aid. This site enables students to apply for student financial aid from the federal government, including the Pell Grant, Perkins Loan, Stafford Loan, and Work-Study. Most important, students can apply electronically for federal student aid by using FAFSA on the Web.

Federal Student Aid, an office of the U.S. Department of Education, plays a central and essential role in America's postsecondary education community. Federal Student Aid's core mission is to ensure that all eligible Americans benefit from federal financial assistance—grants, loans, and work-study programs—for education beyond high school. The programs they administer comprise the nation's largest source of student aid. The staff of 1,100 is based in ten cities in addition to the Washington headquarters.

In overseeing $391 billion of outstanding student loans, it's this organization's job to ensure that all partners in the student aid community—schools, lenders, servicers, and guaranty agencies—operate fairly, honestly, and efficiently. Another key role they perform is to make students and their families aware that financial aid is available and is a necessary first step to further education. As America's premier source of federal student aid information, they distribute numerous publications, host multiple Web sites, and run several customer call centers. Most of these services are provided in Spanish as well.

The Federal Student Aid team is passionately committed to making education beyond high school more attainable for all Americans, regardless of socioeconomic status. By championing access to postsecondary education, they uphold its value as a force for greater inclusion in American society and for the continued vitality of America as a nation.

The National Association of Student Financial Aid Administrators (NASFAA) is an association of 3,000 colleges, universities, career schools, and others with an interest in the effective administration of student financial aid. The Association does not provide financial aid to students. However, NASFAA provides information on the financial aid process and directs students to some of the more important and helpful financial aid guidance on the Web.

U.S. Department of Education provides parents, teachers, students, and administrators with the latest about information centers for financial aid, grants and contracts, policy, programs, and research and statistics. The site also provides links to state departments of education, K–12 schools, school districts, and colleges and universities; other government Web resources; libraries; and education organizations.

4

I Earn Too Much, Now What?

FAST FACTS

➤ **Consider potential debt burden.** Because parents of no-need students are often forced to take on additional loans, "family debt burden" increases. Colleges don't usually talk about this type of debt burden.

➤ **Look for "free money" deals.** There are literally thousands of these types of deals offered by schools across the country.

➤ **Ask your employer if it offers financial aid to students.** Upper-income, high-adjusted gross income (AGI) families should check with their employers to determine whether they offer an education assistance program.

Most people think need is determined by income alone. This is not the case. Take, for instance, an airline pilot who earns $200,000 a year. Based on his annual salary, you'd probably think he can easily afford to pay for his child's college education out of his own pocket. Consider, however, that this same parent has recently remarried, has taken on a "blended" family, and has college financing responsibilities both as a parent and a stepparent. Based on these other circumstances, he surely has "need." Not necessarily, say the federal government and many college and university financial aid offices across the country. So what can "no-need" families do when the dreaded college financial aid analysis letter arrives in the mail stating they earn too much? Plenty.

➢ **Take a practice run.** When your child has selected colleges of interest, visit as many as you can during his or her junior year. During the campus visit, ask the financial aid office to give you an early estimate of your financial aid status. This is good practice in preparation for the real thing during your child's senior year. Solving financial aid issues is important to a successful education, so practice and learn all you need to know while your child is a junior so that you are prepared to make a solid decision the next year.

➢ **Borrow against your home equity.** No-need families may want to look into a home equity loan or a home equity line of credit. A home-equity loan interest rate may hover around 7.5 to 8 percent, while a line of credit could be similar. The advantage is that your interest might be tax deductible. Check with your financial adviser to see if this option is beneficial to you.

➢ **Shop for the best loan.** One year prior to your child's enrollment in college is a good time to shop around and compare the best college loan deals. The private loan college market is very competitive, so do your homework.

➢ **Use education assistance programs.** Another strategy is for upper-income, high-adjusted gross income families to check with their employer to determine whether it offers an education assistance program. If your employer will pay for certain education expenses, you might be able to exclude up to $5,250 of assistance from your taxable income. Check with your financial adviser for details.

BE AWARE OF POTENTIAL DEBT BURDEN

For starters, if you are a no-need family, you'll need to narrow down and focus on probable colleges in which you and your child are interested. You should first consider in-state public colleges since they offer much better tuition rates. Also, loan debt should always be foremost on your mind. If you are denied need-based aid, you most certainly will have to borrow funds, and you'll want to minimize your potential debt burden. Remember that more than 50 percent of students attending postsecondary education take more than four years to earn a bachelor's degree. Therefore, each additional year your child spends in school will add to the debt burden.

It is all too common for both students and parents to borrow at the same time for college expenses. For example, a no-need student can borrow $3,500 in her freshman year, but because she shows no need, a Federal Stafford Loan will be unsubsidized. This means that while she is enrolled in school she must either make interest payments on the loan or allow the interest to capitalize before the repayment period begins. Her parents, knowing that $3,500 isn't nearly enough, will also have to borrow from the federal government and maybe from a private lender as well. This is your "family loan debt burden," and you need to be aware of it as you make decisions.

LOOK FOR "FREE MONEY" DEALS

There are literally thousands of "free money" deals throughout the country, and maybe your list of schools has some. Here are some examples of the great deals offered by a number of colleges, available to everyone, including those who are deemed to have no need:

> ➤ *Academic Scholarships* A minimum high school GPA of 3.0 and a minimum ACT composite score of 20 or SAT composite score of 1730 are required to receive a full-tuition scholarship covering

tuition and required fees and room and board. Students must maintain a GPA of 3.0 to renew the scholarship.

➤ *Presidential Scholarships* These competitive scholarships are available to high school seniors who rank in the upper 25 percent of their graduating class, have a minimum ACT composite score of 20 and a minimum GPA of 3.0, and demonstrate leadership ability. Award amounts vary from $500 to $5,000 per year.

➤ *Honors Program* These scholarships are available to freshmen who have a minimum high school GPA of 3.0 and ACT scores of 28 or SAT scores of 2040 and enroll in the Honors Program. Recipients receive $500 in addition to any other scholarships they have received.

➤ *Trustees' Scholarships* Full-tuition scholarships are awarded to five first-time freshmen with a 3.9 GPA and a minimum score of 2080 on the SAT or 30 on the ACT. The scholarships are renewable for up to four years while in pursuit of a bachelor's degree. Recipients must also maintain a 3.6 GPA.

➤ *Sibling Scholarships* These awards are available to two or more dependent undergraduate siblings attending the same school full-time during the same year. Each sibling receives $1,000 for up to four years.

➤ *President's Emerging Leader Program* Awards of $3,000 per academic year are given to students who demonstrate leadership potential and extracurricular involvement and have a minimum GPA of 3.0. Three letters of recommendation and a personal interview are required for consideration.

These awards represent just a sampling of the many types of "free money" deals available to families. Although such deals are school specific, you can uncover similar deals offered by colleges and universities across the country by doing a little research and asking the right questions.

"LOCK IN" YOUR TUITION/AFFORDABLE PAYMENT PLANS

You should consider state-sponsored savings plans, specifically prepaid tuition plans. Also, some colleges are "locking in" their tuition rates. So if you can afford to pay four years of tuition well in advance of your child's enrollment, this could be an option for you.

Many schools also allow families to pay tuition on a monthly basis. The advantage is the payments are interest free. However, there is an application fee. Check with your school to see what alternative payment plans are available.

5

Scholarships and Grants: Secrets to a Free Ride

FAST FACTS

➢ **Start your search up close and personal.** The most likely source of scholarships for most students is geographically close to home, and the best single identifying source of these local opportunities resides in the high school guidance office.

➢ **Investigate scholarship search services.** If your child is an exceptional student and you feel he or she might qualify for academic scholarship recognition, there are many free scholarship search services available. Avoid offers of guaranteed monies for which you have to pay. Never pay for any service that you can discover on your own for free.

➢ **Find out if the college offers merit aid.** If so, how many merit scholarships does it give? How are they determined, and who determines the recipients?

Non-need-based aid is also referred to as merit-based aid. The qualifications vary from program to program and are usually competitive. Recipients are chosen because of their talent in the particular skills used for selection. Merit-based aid can also be awarded based on involvement in community service, leadership abilities, and fields of study.

Unlike need-based aid, where the federal government provides the majority of funds, there are many sources and many routes you can take to find non-need-based aid. It exists at the federal, state, and institutional levels and can be found in the form of private scholarships, grants, and loans. Whichever route you choose, the best source of information on how to apply for non-need-based aid is the source itself. For example:

> Visit, write, or phone the school at which your child plans to enroll to learn more about the different merit-based programs that may be available.

> Research the Internet and the reference section of your local library for Web sites and books that list scholarship and grant programs, such as *Peterson's Scholarships, Grants & Prizes*.

> Check with your child's high school guidance counselor for information on scholarships and ask for applications.

Regardless of its source, non-need-based aid can often affect eligibility for need-based aid. However, the way it influences other aid differs from school to school. For example, it may reduce the amount of loans you must secure or it may be used to fill the gap, if any, between the amount of need-based aid offered and your actual need. While some schools might reduce certain need-based grants if your child receives other non-need-based grants, the Federal Pell Grant is never reduced.

No matter what the source or type of aid obtained, the financial aid office must be kept informed of any and all outside assistance your child receives. This obligation applies even if you learn about an additional scholarship after receiving formal notification from the school of the aid it plans to offer. The financial aid administrator must take this assistance into account when awarding federal aid.

SCHOLARSHIPS

Scholarships offset or eliminate the climbing cost of college tuition and have turned the dreams of many young students into reality. Those lucky enough to land an award often graduate with little to no debt. It doesn't hurt your pocketbook either, of course, since any dollars your child receives soften the blow to your bank account.

Yet, all too often, families fail to explore awards for which they might be eligible, assuming their household incomes are too high or their kids can't compete with their overachieving classmates. They're making a big mistake.

The word "scholarship" often causes confusion. The definition of scholarship is "free money" given to cover educational costs for under-graduate students. Many people, however, including college financial aid officials and program sponsors, use the word to refer to all forms of student gift aid, including fellowships and grants. Here are some definitions so you are aware of the differences in meaning when you encounter these other terms:

> If applicable, check to see if your child's college offers first-generation scholarships for students whose parents never attended college.

> ➤ *Scholarships and Grants* Gift aid that is used to pay educational costs.

> ➤ *Need-Based Scholarships* Gift aid based on demonstrated need. Need, as defined by colleges and the federal government, is the difference between the cost of attending a college and the EFC.

> ➤ *Merit-Based Scholarships* Financial aid based on criteria other than financial need, including academic major, career goals, grades, test scores, athletic ability, hobbies, talents, place of residence or birth, ethnic identity, religious affiliation, a student's or a parent's military or public safety service, disability, union membership, employment history, community service, or club affiliations.

➤ *Prizes* Money given in recognition of an outstanding achievement. Prizes often are awarded to winners of competitions.

➤ *Internships* A defined period of time working in the intern's field of interest with and under the supervision of the professional staff of a host organization. Interns often work part-time or during the summer. Some internships offer stipends in the form of an hourly wage or fixed allowance.

Use the following checklist when investigating merit scholarships:

☐ *Take advantage of any scholarships for which your child is automatically eligible based on employer benefits, military service, association or church membership, other affiliations, or student or parent attributes (ethnic background, nationality, etc.).*

☐ *Apply for other awards for which your child might be eligible based on the characteristics and affiliations indicated above, but where there is a selection process.*

☐ *Find out if your state has a merit scholarship program.*

☐ *Look into national scholarship competitions.* High school guidance counselors usually know about these scholarships. Examples of these awards are the National Merit® Scholarship, Coca-Cola Scholarship, Thrivent Financial for Lutherans®, Intel Science Talent Search, and the U.S. Senate Youth Program.

☐ *Contact an armed services recruiter or a high school guidance counselor for information about ROTC (Reserve Officers' Training Corps) scholarships offered by the Army, Navy, Marines, and Air Force.* A full ROTC scholarship covers all tuition, fees, and textbook costs. Acceptance of an ROTC scholarship entails, for example, a commitment to take a military science course and to serve as an officer in the sponsoring branch of the service. Competition is heavy, and preference may be given to students in

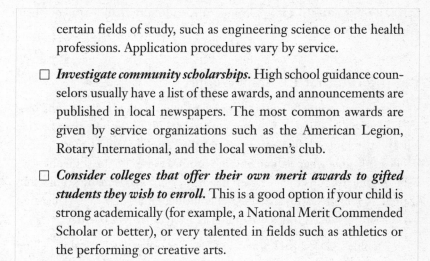

certain fields of study, such as engineering science or the health professions. Application procedures vary by service.

☐ *Investigate community scholarships.* High school guidance counselors usually have a list of these awards, and announcements are published in local newspapers. The most common awards are given by service organizations such as the American Legion, Rotary International, and the local women's club.

☐ *Consider colleges that offer their own merit awards to gifted students they wish to enroll.* This is a good option if your child is strong academically (for example, a National Merit Commended Scholar or better), or very talented in fields such as athletics or the performing or creative arts.

A SCHOLARSHIP ROADMAP

Start Early

Deadlines for scholarships generally don't come due until students become high school seniors. But experts agree that college-bound kids and their parents should start searching for scholarships as early as their freshman year. There are even a number of programs that include separate competitions for grades 7–9. In many of the largest scholarship competitions, students who have not won a top prize can enter each year that they are eligible. For experience alone, it is worthwhile to get involved as a freshman or sophomore. For example, a student who's achieved Eagle Scout status—the top rank in the Boy Scouts of America—would do well to stick with Scouts through high school. That's because the National Eagle Scout Association awards various scholarships, including one that's worth $48,000 and four other $20,000 scholarships. Note that applicants must be a graduating senior or entering college when they apply.

Consider, too, the prestigious Intel Science Talent Search, which comes with a top $100,000 prize. Students must develop and submit their own experiments to be considered for this award. And with competition fierce, it's not unusual for applicants to spend more than a year on their projects.

Let the Internet Be Your Guide

Tracking down scholarships is a lot easier thanks to the Internet. The best Web sites enable students to submit a personal profile online, then receive a list of matching scholarships for which they might qualify. Offer as much detail as possible when submitting the profile. For example, someone who lists "engineering" as their chosen major may not get as many scholarship listings as someone who specifies "chemical engineering." That's because various professional groups use grants as a way to attract talent.

Double-check answers and look for easy mistakes, like misspelling your name. Don't leave answers blank. Students can modify and resubmit their profiles to see what other scholarships match. It's also smart to sign up with at least two sites. You'll find that there's plenty of overlap, but you can rest assured you've identified most of the scholarships available.

Finally, never ever pay fees to obtain a listing. There are enough free databases out there, and paying money to identify grants and awards does not improve the chances of success. In fact, one study by a group of colleges found that less than 1 percent of students using fee-based searches actually won money.

Think Small

It's no surprise that mega-grants, such as the Coca-Cola Scholars Program and the Gates Millennium Scholars Program, have certain appeal. After all, they come with big prizes that add cachet to a student's resume.

But there are good reasons to think small. For starters, thousands of students apply for big-name grants, so competition can be tough. Smaller scholarships that are worth less than $1,000 or grants from community organizations often are easier to obtain. That's also true for scholarships from local groups, such as the Parent-Teacher Association, the area Lions Club, or your local church, mosque, or synagogue. Many employers even offer scholarships for employees' children.

What's more, winning a smaller scholarship may boost your child's chances of snagging something bigger down the road since it indicates that he or she is worthy of an award.

> It is important to remember that even though your child is in college, the scholarship quest has not ended. There are plenty of scholarships specifically geared for college sophomores, juniors, and seniors.

You can find out about local scholarships through a high school college counselor. Another good source is financial aid offices at community colleges, which tend to be good, if not better, about advertising local scholarships.

Minimize Your Efforts/Maximize Your Results

Entering scholarship competitions isn't as much work as it appears to be. Students can make their intellectual and creative efforts work overtime for them. You may find that several contests in one field—such as science, public speaking, the arts, or writing—have similar requirements, and work that was prepared for one contest can often be adapted for use in several others.

Application deadlines do not always fall at convenient times. Be ready for whatever opportunities may become available. If your child is a senior, it's a good idea to keep a file of materials that are often required. By holding on to copies of papers and documents, you can quickly duplicate them and send them off as part of scholarship application forms without wasting valuable time. Keep copies of at least three recommendations on file (from the principal or vice-principal, guidance counselor, and one or more teachers) concerning your child's academic and nonacademic achievements as well as his or her personal qualities. Keep copies of any of your child's general college application essays that can be recycled for scholarship application forms. If your child has a number of impressive achievements in a certain area (debate victories, athletic awards, published newspaper articles, etc.), list and describe them in a one-page write-up that can be added to scholarship forms. If your child is interested in entering writing competitions, keep copies on hand of his or her best work. Time is money—scholarship money.

Obtain and Examine Past Winning Entries

Winners of scholarships in writing or public speaking have often benefited from studying the entries of previous contest winners. Examples can usually be obtained by writing directly to the contest administrators.

Make Friends with Your Guidance Counselor

Have your child talk with his or her counselor at the beginning of the school year and request assistance in your efforts to enter and win competitions. Get copies of all information that the school receives about scholarship opportunities in fields that interest your child.

Use Original Material Only

Plagiarism is the fastest way to be eliminated from a program. Be certain that your child submits his or her own work or gives appropriate credit to material taken from other sources.

Read All Contest Materials Carefully

Although this seems obvious, numerous contest officials have pointed out that many students do not pay attention to the rules. Be sure to obtain a copy of the most recent brochure to get firsthand information about deadlines, correct entry procedures, and scholarship criteria. Don't take someone else's word about contest rules, even that of a well-meaning friend or school adviser.

SCHOLARSHIP SCAMS: WHAT THEY ARE AND WHAT TO WATCH OUT FOR

Several hundred thousand students seek and find scholarships every year. An award from a private source can tilt the scales with respect to a student's ability to attend a specific college during a particular year. Unfortunately, for prospective scholarship seekers, the private aid sector is virtually without patterns or rules. It has, over many years, become a combination of individual programs, each with its own award criteria, timetables, application procedures, and decision-making processes.

Regrettably, the combination of an urgency to locate money, limited time, and this complex and bewildering system has created opportunities for fraud. It has been estimated that for every 10 students who receive a legitimate scholarship, one is victimized by a fraudulent scheme or scam that poses as a legitimate foundation, scholarship sponsor, or scholarship search service. Every year, an estimated 350,000 families are cheated in various scholarship scams, totalling more than $5 million.

These fraudulent businesses advertise in campus newspapers, distribute flyers, mail letters and postcards, provide toll-free phone numbers, and have Web sites. The most obvious frauds operate as scholarship search services or scholarship clearinghouses. Another segment sets up as a scholarship sponsor, pockets the money from the fees that are paid by thousands of hopeful scholarship seekers, and returns little, if anything, in proportion to the amount it collects. A few of these scams inflict great harm by gaining access to individuals' credit or checking accounts with the intent to extort funds.

A typical mode of operation is for for scammers to send out a huge mailing to college and high school students, claiming that the company has either a scholarship or a scholarship list for the students. These companies often provide toll-free numbers. When recipients call, they are told by high-pressure telemarketers that the company has unclaimed scholarships and that for fees ranging from $10 to $400 the callers get back at least $1,000 in scholarship money or the fee will be refunded. Customers who pay, if they receive anything at all, are mailed a list of sources of financial aid that are no better than, and are in many cases inferior to, what can be found in any of the major scholarship guides available in bookstores and libraries or on the Web. The "lucky" recipients have to apply on their own for the scholarships. Many of the programs are contests, loans, or work-study programs rather than gift aid. Some are no longer in existence, have expired deadlines, or set eligibility requirements that students cannot meet. Customers who seek refunds have to demonstrate that they have applied in writing to each source on the list and received a rejection letter from each of them. Frequently, even when customers can provide this almost-impossible-to-obtain proof, refunds are not given. In the worst cases, the companies ask for consumers' checking account or credit card numbers and take funds without authorization.

The Federal Trade Commission (FTC) warns students and their parents to be wary of fraudulent search services that promise to do all the work for you.

"Bogus scholarship search services are just a variation of the 'you have won' prize-promotion scam, targeted to a particular audience—students and parents who are anxious about paying for college," said Jodie Bernstein, former director of the FTC's Bureau of Consumer Protection. "They guarantee students and their families free scholarship money . . . all they have to do to claim it is pay an up-front fee."

There are legitimate scholarship search services. However, a scholarship search service cannot truthfully guarantee that a student will receive a scholarship, and students almost always will fare as well or better by doing their own homework using a reliable scholarship information source, such as *Peterson's Scholarships, Grants & Prizes*, than by wasting time and more importantly money with a search service that promises a scholarship.

The FTC warns scholarship seekers to be alert for these seven warning signs of a scam:

1. **"This scholarship is guaranteed or your money back."** No service can guarantee that it will get you a grant or scholarship. Refund guarantees often have impossible conditions attached. Review a service's refund policies in writing before you pay a fee. Typically, fraudulent scholarship search services require that applicants show rejection letters from each of the sponsors on the list they provide. If a sponsor no longer exists, if it really does not provide scholarships, or if it has a rolling application deadline, letters of rejection are almost impossible to obtain.

2. **"The scholarship service will do all the work."** Unfortunately, nobody else can fill out the personal information forms, write the essays, and supply the references that many scholarships may require.

3. **"The scholarship will cost some money."** Be wary of any charges related to scholarship information services or individual scholarship applications, especially in significant amounts. Some legitimate scholarship sponsors charge fees to defray their processing expenses. True scholarship sponsors, however, should distribute money, not make it from application fees. Before you send money to apply for a scholarship, investigate the sponsor.

4. **"You can't get this information anywhere else."** In addition to Peterson's, scholarship directories from other publishers are available in any large bookstore, public library, or high school guidance office.

5. **"You are a finalist"—in a contest you never entered, or "You have been selected by a national foundation to receive a scholarship."** Most legitimate scholarship programs almost never seek out particular applicants. Most scholarship sponsors will only contact you in response to an inquiry. Most lack the budget and mandate to do anything more than this. If you think that there is any real possibility that you may have been selected to receive a scholarship, before you send any money investigate to make sure the sponsor or program is legitimate.

6. **"The scholarship service needs your credit card or checking account number in advance."** *Never provide your credit card or bank account number over the telephone to the representative of an organization that you do not know.* A legitimate need-based scholarship program will not ask for your checking account number. Get information in writing first. **Note:** An unscrupulous operation does not need your signature on a check. It schemes to set up situations that allow it to drain a victim's account with unauthorized withdrawals.

7. **"You are invited to a free seminar (or interview) with a trained financial aid consultant who will unlock the secrets of how to make yourself eligible for more financial aid."** Sometimes, these consultants offer some good tips on preparing for college, but often they are trying to get you to sign up for a long-term contract for services you don't need. Often, these

"consultants" are trying to sell you other financial products, such as annuities, life insurance, or other financial services that have little to do with financial aid. By doing your own research with books from Peterson's or other respected organizations, using the Web, and working with your high school guidance office and the college financial aid office, you will get all the help you need to ensure you have done a thorough job of preparing for the financing of your child's college education.

In addition to the FTC's seven warning signs, here are some other points to keep in mind when considering a scholarship program:

➢ **Fraudulent scholarship operations often use official-sounding names containing words such as federal, national, administration, division, federation, and foundation.** Their names often are a slight variation of the name of a legitimate government or private organization. Do not be fooled by a name that seems reputable or official, an official-looking seal, or a Washington, D.C., address.

➢ **If your child wins a scholarship, you will receive official written notification by mail, not over the telephone.** Sponsors who do call to inform you will follow up with a letter in the mail. If a request for money is made over the phone, the operation is probably fraudulent.

➢ **Be wary if an organization's address is a post office box number or a residential address.** If a bona fide scholarship program uses a post office box number, it usually will include a street address and telephone number on its stationery.

➢ **Beware of telephone numbers with a 900, 809, 758, or 664 area codes.** These may charge you a fee of several dollars a minute for a call that could be a long recording that provides only a list of addresses or names.

➢ **A dishonest operation may put pressure on an applicant by claiming that awards are on a first-come, first-served basis.** Some scholarship programs give preference to early applicants. However, if you are told, especially over the telephone, that you must respond quickly, but you will not hear about the results for several months, there may be a problem.

> **Be wary of endorsements.** Fraudulent operations claim endorsements by groups with names similar to well-known private or government organizations. The Better Business Bureau (BBB) and other government agencies do not endorse businesses.

If an organization requires that you pay something for a scholarship and you have never heard of it before and cannot verify that it is a legitimate operation, the best advice is to pay nothing. If you have already paid money to such an organization and find reason to doubt its legitimacy, call your bank to stop payment on your check, if possible, or call your credit card company and tell it that you think you were the victim of consumer fraud.

To find out how to recognize, report, and stop a scholarship scam, contact:

Federal Trade Commission
Consumer Response Center
600 Pennsylvania Avenue, N.W.
Washington, D.C. 20580
Web site: www.ftc.gov

The Better Business Bureau (BBB) maintains files of businesses about which it has received complaints. You should call both your local BBB office and the BBB office where the organization in question is located; each local BBB has different records. Call 703-276-0100 to get the telephone number of your local BBB. The national address is:

The Council of Better Business Bureaus
4200 Wilson Boulevard, Suite 800
Arlington, VA 22203-1838
Web site: www.bbb.org

There are many wonderful scholarships available to qualified students who spend the time and effort to locate and apply for them. However, we advise you to exercise caution in using scholarship search services and, when you must pay money, always use careful judgment when considering a scholarship program's sponsor.

INSTITUTION-BASED GIFT AID

College need-based scholarships are frequently figured into a student's financial aid package. Most colleges award both need- and merit-based scholarships, although a small number (most notably Ivy League colleges) offer only need-based scholarships. Colleges may offer merit-based scholarships to freshmen with specific academic strengths, talents in the creative or performing arts, special achievements or activities, and a wide variety of particular circumstances. Some of these circumstances are: parents in specific professions; residents of particular geographic areas; spouses, children, and siblings of other students; and students with disabilities. A college's financial aid office can inform you about the need-based scholarships they offer.

Merit scholarships have become ubiquitous. Usually, the admissions office is the main source of information about any merit-based scholarships the college offers. Some colleges have information about their scholarships on their Web sites.

ATHLETIC SCHOLARSHIPS

Whether a student is interested in baseball, basketball, crew, cross-country, fencing, field hockey, football, golf, gymnastics, lacrosse, sailing, skiing, soccer, softball, swimming and diving, tennis, track and field, volleyball, or wrestling, scholarship dollars may be available. But you and your child must plan ahead if you want to get his or her tuition paid for in return for competitive abilities.

At the beginning of your child's junior year in high school, ask his or her guidance counselor to help you make sure the required number and mix of academic courses are taken. Also find out the SAT and ACT score minimums that must be met to play college sports. Ask the counselor about grade requirements since a student must be certified by the NCAA Initial Eligibility Clearinghouse. This process must begin by the end of junior year by submitting a Student Release Form (available in the guidance office). You can find the latest NCAA eligibility requirements from the guidance counselor.

But before you do all that, think. Does your child want and need an athletic scholarship? Certainly it is prestigious to receive an athletic scholarship, but some athletes compare having an athletic scholarship to having a job. Meetings, training sessions, practices, games, and studying take away from social and leisure time. Also, with very few full-ride scholarships available, your child will most likely receive a partial scholarship or a one-year renewable contract. If the scholarship is not renewed, you may be left scrambling for financial aid. So ask yourself and your child if you are ready for the demands and roles associated with accepting an athletic scholarship.

Types of Athletic Scholarships

Colleges and universities offer two basic types of athletic scholarships:

1. The *institutional* grant, which is an agreement between the athlete and the college

2. The *conference* grant, which also binds the college to the athlete

The difference between the two is that the athlete who signs an institutional grant can change his or her mind and sign with another team. The athlete who signs a conference contract cannot renegotiate another contract with a school that honors conference grants.

Here are the various ways a scholarship may be offered:

➤ *Full Four-Year* Also known as full ride, these scholarships pay for room, board, tuition, and books. Due to the high cost of awarding scholarships, this type of grant is being discouraged by conferences around the country in favor of the one-year renewable contract or the partial scholarship.

➤ *Full One-Year Renewable Contract* This type of scholarship, which has basically replaced the full four-year grant, is automatically renewed at the end of each school year for four years if the conditions of the contract are met. The recruiter will probably tell your child in good faith that the intent is to offer a four-year scholarship, but he is legally only allowed to offer a one-year grant. You must ask the recruiter as well as other players what the record has been of renewing scholarships for athletes who comply athletically, academically, and socially.

➤ *One-Year Trial Grant (Full or Partial)* This is a verbal agreement between the student and the institution that, at the end of the year, renewal will be dependent upon the student's academic and athletic performance.

➤ *Partial Scholarship* The partial grant is for any part of the total cost of college. The student may be offered room and board but not tuition and books, or he or she may be offered just tuition. The possibility exists to negotiate to a full scholarship after the freshman year.

➤ *Waiver of Out-of-State Fees* This award is for out-of-state students to attend a college or university at the same tuition as an in-state student.

Finding and Getting Athletic Scholarships

Here are four steps to help your child snag that scholarship:

1. **Contact the school formally.** Once your child has made a list of schools he or she is interested in (check out *Peterson's Sports Scholarships & College Athletic Programs* to help formulate this list), get the names of the head coaches and have your child write a letter to the top twenty schools on the list. With the letter include a factual resume of his or her athletic and academic accomplishments, 10–15 minutes of video highlights of his or her athletic performance (with the player's jersey number noted), and letters of recommendation from his or her high school coach and off-season coach. Also include a season schedule.

2. **Ace the interview.** Before your child meets a recruiter or coach, stress to him or her the importance of exhibiting self-confidence by using a firm handshake, maintaining eye contact, and being well groomed. According to recruiters, the most effective attitude is quiet confidence, respect, sincerity, and enthusiasm.

3. **Ask good questions.** Don't be afraid to probe a recruiter by getting answers to the following questions: Does my child qualify athletically and academically? If he or she is recruited, what would the parameters of the scholarship be? For what position is he or she being considered? It's okay to ask the recruiter to declare what level of interest he or she has in your child.

4. **Follow-up.** Persistence pays off when it comes to seeking an athletic scholarship. And timing can be everything. There are four good times when a follow-up letter to a coach or a personal letter from the student is extremely effective. These are prior to the senior season, during or just after the senior season, just prior to or after announced signing dates (conference-affiliated or national association), and mid- to late summer, in case scholarship offers have been withdrawn or declined.

STATE AND LOCAL SCHOLARSHIPS

Each state government has established one or more financial aid programs for qualified students. Usually, only legal residents of the state are eligible to benefit from such programs. However, some programs are available to out-of-state students attending colleges within the state. States may also offer internship or work-study programs, graduate fellowships and grants, or low-interest loans in addition to grant and forgivable loan programs.

Many states are trying to encourage students to enter specific occupational fields where a shortage of trained personnel exists. Examples are education, science, nursing, and medicine. To attract individuals to these fields, more and more states now provide special loan assistance to students who promise to work in these areas after graduation. If your child accepts such assistance, he or she should confirm whether there is a service obligation as part of the award.

> Almost anyone can find awards that fit his or her individual circumstances.

If you are interested in learning more about state-sponsored programs, the state higher education office should be able to provide information. Brochures and application forms for state scholarship programs are usually available in your child's high school guidance office or from a college financial aid office in your state. Increasingly, state government agencies are putting state scholarship information on their Web sites. The financial aid page of state-administered college or university sites frequently has a list of state-sponsored scholarships and financial aid programs.

Businesses, community service clubs, and local organizations often sponsor scholarship programs for residents of a specific town or county. These can be attractive to a scholarship seeker because the odds of winning can be higher than they would be for scholarships drawing from a wider pool of applicants. However, because the information network at the local level is spotty, it is often difficult to find information about their existence. Some of the best sources of information about these local programs are high school guidance offices, community college financial aid offices, high school district administrative offices, and public libraries.

PRIVATE AID

Billions of dollars every year are given by private donors to students and their families to help with the expenses of a college education. In the past, non-institutional and non-government sponsors gave more than $3 billion in financial aid to help undergraduate students pay for college costs. Foundations, fraternal and ethnic organizations, community service clubs, churches and religious groups, philanthropies, companies and industry groups, labor unions and public employees' associations, veterans' groups, trusts, and bequests all make up a large network of possible sources.

It is always worthwhile to look into these scholarships. It is especially important for those who do not qualify for need-based financial aid, students and families who wish to supplement the aid being given by governmental or university sources, and students who possess special abilities, achievements, or personal qualifications (e.g., memberships in church or civic organizations, specific ethnic backgrounds, parents who served in the armed forces, etc.) that fit the criteria of one or more of the various private scholarship sponsors.

Some factors that can affect eligibility for these awards are beyond your control, such as ethnic heritage. Other factors, such as academic, scientific, technological, athletic, artistic, or creative merit, are not easily or quickly met unless the student has previously committed to a particular endeavor. However, eligibility for many programs is within your control if you plan ahead. For example, your child can start or keep up current membership in a church or civic organization, par-

> Ask your employer(s), union, and any community clubs to which you belong if they offer financial aid to students.

ticipate in volunteer service efforts, or pursue an interest, from amateur radio to golf to raising animals to writing and more. Any of these actions might give him or her an edge for a particular scholarship or grant opportunity.

VETERANS EDUCATIONAL BENEFITS

The Department of Veterans Affairs and the Department of Defense administer several educational assistance programs for veterans and their dependents.

The Survivors' and Dependents' Educational Assistance Program (DEA) provides benefits to children and spouses of veterans who died or were permanently disabled as a result of a service-related injury. Under the DEA, dependents between the ages of 18 and 26 may receive a stipend (prorated for less-than-full-time enrollment) at the completion of each month of study. This monthly stipend from the Department of Veterans Affairs helps to cover education and personal expenses that are incurred while the student is enrolled at a postsecondary school. Note that these benefits must be considered as a resource by the aid administrator when a student's eligibility for federal, state, and institutional assistance is determined.

Veterans benefits are paid to students for the following types of education programs:

➤ Undergraduate and graduate-degree programs

➤ Cooperative training programs

➤ Accredited independent study programs leading to a college degree

➤ Courses leading to a certificate or diploma from business, technical, or vocational schools

➤ Apprenticeships or job-training programs offered by a company or union

➤ Farm cooperative courses

➤ Study-abroad programs that lead to a college degree

Additional information regarding these and other veteran educational benefits may be obtained from the nearest office of the Department of Veterans Affairs or by accessing their Web site at www.va.gov. You can also call or write the nearest VA office for pamphlets and brochures. Most colleges and universities have either a VA office or someone on staff who handles most VA eligibility issues and can help you through the process. If you are unsure about who to talk to, ask the financial aid office for assistance.

VOCATIONAL REHABILITATION FOR THE DISABLED

Access to educational opportunities for individuals with disabilities is guaranteed through federal laws governing vocational rehabilitation. Federal allocations are provided to each state on a matching basis to assist people with disabilities who have employment potential but whose impairments create barriers to that employment.

Vocational rehabilitation programs also provide comprehensive services under an individualized written rehabilitation plan. The plan can include evaluation, vocational training, special devices required for employment, job placement, and follow-up services. Some states offer educational assistance programs to disabled students through agencies known as Offices of Vocational Rehabilitation (OVR). While students with disabilities may participate in any of the federal financial aid programs, additional aid through vocational rehabilitation programs can be used to pay for unique expenses incurred due to a disability. Eligible students can also receive funds for tuition, fees, books and supplies, and maintenance and transportation allowances. If your child is disabled, contact your state department of vocational rehabilitation for further information.

CHAPTER

6

Saving

FAST FACTS

> **If you haven't started any kind of savings for college, start putting some money aside now.** The money you put in the bank today can be used as a resource for college. More importantly, you have created an on-going resource in your family budget that can be used for a loan payment or monthly payment plan when your child is in college.

> **Reduce your child's savings.** If you have shifted significant resources into your children's names to lessen your federal income tax burden, this could reduce your children's financial aid eligibility. In the calculations for financial aid eligibility, the student's savings are assessed at a much higher rate than those savings reported for parents. If you or your child have set aside funds for college expenses, consider using those savings to pay for necessary college expenses—perhaps a new vehicle or prepayment of tuition and fees—prior to filling out the needs analysis form. It might make a significant difference, particularly if those expenditures reduce the student's savings.

In an economy where the only economic constant is inconsistency, you may be worrying about how far your tuition nest egg will take you. Stay calm. There are factors working in your favor. For one thing, new tax rules have kicked in, allowing you to save more of your money tax-free. However, knowing where to save your pennies and how to search for free money will start you on the right path.

Here's a look at the three most popular ways to save—Coverdell Education Saving Accounts, 529s, and custodial accounts—and how they affect your financial aid eligibility.

COVERDELL ESAs: NEW AND IMPROVED

Let's start with Education IRAs, which have officially been renamed the Coverdell Education Savings Accounts (ESAs). ESAs have recently become a more attractive education-savings vehicle, especially for families in the higher tax brackets. The Economic Growth and Tax Relief Reconcilliation Act of 2001 raised the maximum annual ESA contribution to $2,000 per child, up from a measly $500. And it raised the income eligibility limit for married couples wishing to open an account to $220,000 a year. If your adjusted gross income is between $190,000 and $220,000 (for joint filers), the amount you can contribute is gradually reduced. Also, under the new tax rules, you will no longer be penalized for contributing to both an ESA and a 529 in the same year for the same beneficiary.

Contributions to an ESA are not tax deductible, but they grow tax free. You can invest your contributions any way you wish, but withdrawals must be used for qualified education expenses, the definition of which was broadened by the Economic Growth and Tax Relief Reconcilliation Act of 2001. In addition to using ESA money to pay for college, families can now use it to pay for tuition at elementary and secondary schools, as well as ancillary expenses, such as tutoring or computers. A Coverdell ESA account held in the student's name is more likely to reduce the student's eligibility for financial aid than a Coverdell ESA account held in an adult parent or guardian's name.

Here is a brief overview of the pros and cons of Education Savings Accounts.

Advantages of Education Savings Accounts

> ➤ Withdrawals that are used to pay the beneficiary's qualified education expenses are completely income-tax free at the federal level.

> ➤ Qualified education expenses include elementary and secondary school expenses.

> ➤ You have complete freedom to choose your own investment portfolio.

> ➤ You can change the beneficiary without penalty if certain conditions are met.

> ➤ You can contribute to an ESA and a 529 Plan in the same year for the same beneficiary without triggering a penalty.

> ➤ The account is treated as an asset of the parent for federal financial aid purposes and assessed at a rate of up to 5.6 percent if the parent is the owner of the account or plan. It is not considered an asset of a dependent student.

Disadvantages of Education Savings Accounts

> ➤ You can contribute a maximum of only $2,000 per year.

> ➤ Your ability to contribute depends on your income—to make the full $2,000 contribution, single filers must have a modified adjusted gross income (MAGI) of $110,000 or less, and joint filers must have a MAGI of $220,000 or less.

> ➤ Contributions aren't allowed after the beneficiary reaches age 18, unless the beneficiary has special needs.

> ➤ The account must be closed after the beneficiary reaches age 30, unless the beneficiary has special needs.

> Withdrawals from an ESA that are not used for the beneficiary's qualified education expenses are taxed and penalized (the earnings portion of the withdrawal is taxed at the rate of the person who receives the withdrawal and is subject to a 10 percent federal penalty).

529 PLANS: THE HIGH-OCTANE, TAX-FREE CHOICE

529 Plans offer some of the biggest tax breaks around. Money in these accounts now grows completely free of federal tax, as long as it's spent for higher education purposes. Contributions are tax deductible in many states.

For high-income families who are not eligible for Education Savings Accounts, 529s are a great option. There are no income limits, you can contribute up to $12,000 per year without triggering the gift tax (married couples can contribute up to $24,000 by electing to split the gifts), and the lifetime contribution limits to a plan are much higher, exceeding $200,000 in some states. Middle-income families can also benefit from tax-free compounding. 529 Plans are run by the states, so it's important to research the rules that apply in each state.

Prepaid Tuition Plans

Prepaid tuition plans, of course, are also looking like a pretty good bet these days. Such plans allow you to buy education contracts, or units, at today's prices, to be used for tuition some time in the future. In essence, you lock in tomorrow's college costs today. Not a bad deal considering that tuition rates have been rising two to three times faster than the Consumer Price Index since 1980.

As a type of 529 Plan, earnings in prepaid accounts are exempt from federal income tax, and contributions are tax deductible in many states. Traditionally, prepaid plans have been sponsored by individual states and designed to pay for tuition at public institutions within that state. Most are still limited to state residents, but many states have taken steps to become more competitive with 529 Plans. For example, many states now pay a minimum interest rate on prepaid contracts, which guarantees some return even in the unlikely event that tuition prices don't go up. And some are giving full refunds to participants who pull their money out of the plans. States have also made it easier to convert their prepaid contracts to tuition at private schools and schools outside of the state.

Private Schools Get in on the Act

While prepaid plans continue to evolve on the state level, private schools have been given the green light to offer their own such deals. Under the 2001 Tax Relief Act, withdrawals from a private school's prepaid plan became exempt from federal taxes as of 2004.

Hundreds of private schools, ranging from liberal arts schools like Ripon College in Wisconsin to well-known universities like Princeton and the University of Chicago, have joined a consortium of schools called Independent 529 Plan. Parents can buy prepaid contracts good for tuition at any of the member schools. This program is open to all students and has a contribution limit of $177,500 (the equivalent of five years of tuition and mandatory fees at the most expensive member college). If your child does not end up going to one of the schools in the network, you will get a refund of your contributions plus or minus 2 percent for each year in the plan, depending how underlying investments fared.

Frequently Asked Questions About 529 Plans

Q. What is a 529 Plan?

A. In 1996, federal law authorized the Qualified Tuition Program to allow for tax-deferred growth on savings for higher education costs. The term "529" represents the section of the IRS code holding the details. The plans are established and maintained at the state government level. There are two types of plans: the college savings plan and the prepaid college tuition plan.

Q. I thought 529 Plans were tax free. Why do I often hear the term "tax deferred"?

A. 529 Plans were established as tax-deferred higher education savings plans. In 2001, Congress agreed to make them temporarily tax free. After 2010, the gains will be taxable unless Congress extends the law.

Q. Is the tax-free advantage the main reason for the popularity of these plans?

A. The tax-free issue is an important selling point, but parents need to understand that the plans are usually "sold." The state governments sponsor their own plan, advertise the plan to residents, and support the plan with an entire organization of employees. In addition, financial industry professionals (independent or not) sell the parent on saving for college in these type of plans.

Q. What are the consequences of removing my money from a 529 Plan?

A. Currently, the assets in a 529 grow tax-deferred and gains are taken tax free. However, if a family changes its mind and wants to get out of a 529 Plan, the distribution is taxed at the current tax rate of the owner and incurs a 10 percent penalty.

Q. How do I get started?

A. Families can complete the research via the Internet, contact the state 529 Plan office, or contact a financial adviser.

Q. I know I'm keeping this plan for the long term, but can I change from one plan to another—like rolling over a retirement plan?

A. Program changes are allowed, but limited. For example, a family can move (rollover) the savings from one 529 Plan to another only once during a 12-month period while keeping the same beneficiary. A family can also rollover the 529 Plan from one beneficiary to another in the same family as many times as it likes during a 12-month period.

Q. Suppose I'm not interested in changing plans but I want to change my investment strategy. I can do that all I want, right?

A. Actually, no. Account owners can only make one investment strategy change per calendar year or whenever there is a change in a beneficiary. If a family wants more flexibility in its investment strategy, it should consider something other than a 529 Plan.

Advantages of 529 and Prepaid Tuition Plans

➤ People of all income levels are eligible to contribute to a 529 Plan.

➤ 529 Plans have high contribution limits (most plans have contribution limits of $250,000 and up).

➤ Most state savings plans are open to residents of any state.

➤ You can generally open a 529 account after your child reaches age 18.

➤ Plan contributions grow income-tax deferred.

➤ Withdrawals that are used to pay the beneficiary's qualified education expenses are completely income-tax free at the federal level.*

➤ States may offer their own income tax incentives, such as a tax deduction for contributions or a tax exemption for withdrawals used to pay the beneficiary's qualified education expenses.

➤ Plan contributions qualify for the $12,000 ($24,000 for joint gifts) annual gift tax exclusion, and a special election lets you contribute up to $60,000 ($120,000 for joint gifts) in a single year and avoid gift tax by treating the amount as a gift over five years.

➤ Plan contributions aren't considered part of your estate for federal tax purposes, yet you retain control of the account during your lifetime as the account owner.

➤ You can change the beneficiary without penalty if certain conditions are met.

➤ You can contribute to a 529 Plan and an ESA in the same year for the same beneficiary without triggering a penalty.

➤ Once every 12 months you can roll over the beneficiary's 529 account to a different 529 Plan for the same beneficiary without tax or penalty implications.

➤ Some state 529 Plans allow you to change your investment portfolio once each calendar year and/or any time you change the beneficiary.

➤ A 529 account owned by someone other than the parent (such as a grandparent) is not considered an asset of the parent for financial aid purposes.

Disadvantages of 529 Plans and Prepaid Tuition Plans

➤ 529 Plans charge various fees and expenses to cover investment expenses and the administration of your account.

➤ Withdrawals from a 529 Plan that are not used for the beneficiary's qualified education expenses are taxed and penalized (the earnings portion of the withdrawal is subject to a 10 percent federal penalty and is taxed at the income tax-rate of the person who receives the withdrawal).

➤ For state savings plans, your investment choices, if any, are limited to the preestablished investment portfolios offered by the plan; prepaid tuition plans allow you no opportunity to choose your investments.

➤ You are generally limited to the prepaid tuition plan offered by your state of residence.

➤ Prepaid tuition plans are generally designed to pay the undergraduate tuition (but not room and board) costs at in-state public colleges, so the beneficiary won't get the maximum benefits under the plan if he or she attends a private or out-of-state college.

*The provisions of the Economic Growth and Tax Relief Reconciliation Act of 2001 that made qualified withdrawals from a 529 Plan tax free at the federal level will expire on December 31, 2010. Unless Congress extends the law, after December 31, 2010, the federal tax treatment of 529 Plans will revert to the law in effect prior to January 1, 2002.

➤ 529 Plans generally require that all tuition credits be used before the beneficiary reaches age 30 and all withdrawals be completed within 10 years of the time the beneficiary starts college.

➤ When a parent is the owner of a state savings plan account, the account is considered the parent's asset for federal financial aid purposes and is assessed at a rate of 5.6 percent.

➤ State savings plans don't guarantee your return—you could lose some of the money you've contributed.

➤ For state savings plans, states aren't legally required to let you change the investment option on your existing contributions once per calendar year or allow you to choose a new investment option for any future contributions (though most plans do give you this flexibility).

CUSTODIAL ACCOUNTS

The change in tax rules did not make changes to custodial accounts, known as Uniform Transfers to Minors Act accounts (UTMAs) or Uniform Gifts to Minors Act accounts (UGMAs). Compared with the souped-up 529s and ESAs, UTMAs and UGMAs now look less attractive.

A potential lack of control over how the money is used is another drawback for parents. Unlike money from a 529 Plan or ESA, money in an UGMA or UTMA does not have to be used for educational purposes. And since your child gains control of the account when he or she reaches the age of maturity (typically 18), you won't have any say in the matter if the money is spent on something other than college.

It's little wonder, then, that many families are looking for ways to undo their custodial accounts. Many but not all 529 Plans allow transfers from custodial accounts, according to SavingforCollege.com, but they only accept cash, which means any investments in an existing UGMA or UTMA would have to be liquidated before transfer.

For families who maintain a custodial account but will be seeking financial aid, it may be wise to reduce the account before college rolls around. You can legally spend the assets on anything that benefits your child, including private school tuition, an SAT prep course, or a computer.

> No matter what vehicle you use to save for college, be sure to regularly review your overall investing strategy.

If, however, your child is well under 14 and you have only a small amount invested (too small to make it worth the hassle of transferring to a 529 Plan), let the account ride for a while. You can then invest just enough to earn up to the $750 a year in tax-free income allowed.

Following is a brief overview of the pros and cons of custodial accounts.

Advantages of Custodial Accounts

➢ People of all income levels are eligible to open an UGMA/UTMA account.

➢ You can invest as much as you want in an UGMA/UTMA account—there are no contribution limits.

➢ The investments you can contribute to the account are virtually unlimited (though an UTMA account generally gives you more options than an UGMA account).

➢ When your child is age 14 and older, the investment earnings are taxed at your child's income tax rate, not yours.

➢ The account is an asset of the parent if the student is a dependent student, regardless of whether the student or the parent owns the account.

Disadvantages of Custodial Accounts

➢ Investment earnings are generally subject to federal and state income tax every year, and the sale of assets may trigger capital gains tax.

➤ When your child is under age 14, the investment earnings are taxed at your income tax rate, pursuant to the child tax rules.

➤ Gifts made to an UGMA/UTMA account are irrevocable gifts to your child, and withdrawals from the account can be made only for purposes that directly benefit your child.

➤ You can't change the beneficiary.

➤ When the child reaches the age of majority (either 18 or 21, as defined by state law), the child has the right to complete control of the funds.

➤ The account is treated as an asset of the independent child for federal financial aid purposes and is assessed at a rate of 20 percent.

➤ When total contributions exceed $12,000 ($24,000 for joint gifts) in a calendar year, a federal gift tax results.

College Savings Vehicles Compared

	529 Plans	Coverdell ESA	Custodial Account
Participation restrictions	Contributions up to $12,000 a year to a child's 529 account without triggering the gift tax; or a lump sum $60,000 contribution, also without tax impact	Income limit for contributions and $2,000 maximum annual contribution	No
Tax-exempt withdrawals (exempt from federal income tax if used for qualified education expenses)	Yes* (withdrawals may also be exempt from state income tax, depending on state law)	Yes (withdrawals may also be exempt from state income tax, depending on state law)	No
Penalties (when funds aren't used for child's qualified education expenses)	Yes, a 10 percent federal penalty applies to the earnings portion of all nonqualified withdrawals	Same as 529 Plans	No, but withdrawals from the account can only be made for the child's benefit
Financial aid treatment of asset for federal financial aid purposes—assets attributed to the child are weighed more heavily, resulting in less financial aid	State savings plan: parent's asset (if parent is account owner) Prepaid tuition plan: Value is equal to refund value of any credits or certificates purchased	Reported as an asset of parent if the parent is the owner. Not considered a student asset if student is dependent. Value is equal to current balance of the account.	Reported as an asset of parent if the parent is the owner. Not considered a student asset if student is dependent. Value is equal to current balance of the account.
Fees and expenses	State savings plan: typically an annual maintenance fee, an administration fee, and investment expenses based on a percentage of total account value Prepaid tuition plan: typically an enrollment fee and various administrative fees	Depending on the financial institution, there may be fees associated with opening and/or maintaining a Coverdell ESA	Depending on the financial institution, there may be fees associated with opening and/or maintaining a custodial account

*The provisions of the Economic Growth and Tax Relief Reconciliation Act of 2001 that raised the annual contribution limit for Coverdell ESAs to $2,000 and made qualified withdrawals from a 529 Plan tax free at the federal level will expire on December 31, 2010. Unless Congress extends the law, after December 31, 2010, the annual contribution limit for Coverdell ESAs and the federal tax treatment of 529 Plans will revert to the law in effect prior to January 1, 2002.

SAVE WITH U.S. BONDS

An increasing number of states have sanctioned savings plans through bond sales. The savings instrument might be zero-coupon bonds or general obligation bonds. Conditions vary from state to state, so check with your state agency for more details. Under federal tax law, individuals who purchase Series EE U.S. Savings Bonds on or after January 1, 1990, can exclude from taxation all or part of the interest earned on those bonds, subject to certain limitations, if they are paying qualified education expenses (i.e., tuition and fees for themselves, their spouse, or their dependents).

TAKE NOTE OF TIMING

As the college years approach, if you anticipate needing financial aid, strategize the timing of your college savings withdrawals, since aid decisions are based on your financials in the tax year before the school year in which the aid is used.

One of the key strategies is to keep your income as low as possible since income is a heavily weighted factor in needs assessment—up to 47 percent of parental income is considered eligible to pay for school costs. As such, try not to incur capital gains in the tax year before aid is needed. Capital gains count both as income and as an asset—a double-whammy.

No matter what vehicles you use to save for college, be sure to regularly review your overall investing strategy. Your plan should take into account your children's ages, the anticipated tuition costs when your kids matriculate, and whether or not you expect to need financial aid. But perhaps what is most important is that the amount you earmark for college should never, in any way, jeopardize what you need to save for retirement.

Your child can draw on plenty of resources to pay for school, but no one's going to give you a scholarship to retire. Saving for your retirement should always take priority. And the good news is a fat nest egg will not reduce your child's aid eligibility. Financial aid formulas do not take your 401(k) and IRA savings into account.

A PENNY SAVED IS A PENNY NOT BORROWED

If you're behind your savings goal, the expense that lies ahead may look daunting. But that doesn't mean you should not save at all. A little bit goes a long way. By saving just $350 a month for one year, you would have enough to cover tuition costs for one year at a public university. The same savings strategy would cover more than four years of books and school supplies for your child, which average about $900 per year.

And don't forget that saving doesn't end on the first day of college. In fact, if you think your child will qualify for subsidized student loans, your goal may not be to save for college per se, but to help your child pay these loans once interest and monthly payments kick in after graduation.

To make room in your household budget for savings, study your last six months of expenses to see how much you spend in a given month compared with your income. Once you know where your money goes, you can look for places to cut back. Next, set up a regular savings plan and have the money automatically drafted from your checking account each month.

If your child is going to need the college savings in less than than five years, put the money in a money market account or AAA-rated government bond fund. With such a short time horizon, you cannot speculate on the stock market. If you have more than five years, consider investing in a conservative portfolio of stocks and bonds. And remember, don't put any money in your child's name, lest it be considered his or her asset for financial aid formulas.

7

Trimming College Costs

FAST FACTS

➤ **The College-Level Examination Program (CLEP) allows students to demonstrate their proficiency at the college level.** By doing so, it allows the college to exempt the student from college courses (save money), lets students advance to higher-level courses to complete the college requirements earlier (save more money), and exempts students from taking prerequisites or introductory courses (save even more money).

➤ **The Advanced Placement (AP) program allows students to experience college-level work while still in high school.** Many colleges give credit or advanced placement to students who receive "qualifying grades" on AP exams.

➤ **A portion of tuition costs may qualify as a tax credit for parents and/or students contingent upon income and the method of payment.** The Hope Scholarship Credit allows deductions on a per-student basis for the freshman and sophomore years of postsecondary education, while the Lifetime Learning Credit is used on an annual tax-return basis and covers a more expansive timeframe and array of educational courses. Tax-free grants, scholarships, and employer-education assistance used to meet education expenses are not eligible for either tax credit. Education expenses paid for with loans are eligible.

When it comes to paying for school, resourcefulness is as important as resources. The shift away from federal support of grant funds created an environment where loans are the most prevalent form of financial aid. Borrowing means deferring payment for something that you want now. Simply signing on the bottom line of a loan form is the quickest and, unfortunately, easiest way to get money for education. But it can be costly, so you should look for other resources and ways to reduce costs.

CAN YOU REDUCE YOUR BUDGET?

Just as increasing resources is one way to meet need, so is reducing your budget. Packaging of aid by the school is based on the school's definition of cost, which involves some assumptions and averaging. The standard nature of the budget means that it is designed for a typical student with average needs. Your child may actually spend more or less than the budget allows, but this individual variation generally does not affect the amount of aid the school offers. A standard budget assumes that you limit expenditures to reasonable levels. Your child is not expected to live below the poverty level, but he or she is expected to accept some sacrifices in order to obtain an education. To determine whether these standard costs can be reduced, you must examine them carefully and then examine your child's level of expectations about living on limited means.

> Cost of Attendance is frequently referred to as the student budget, and it takes into consideration expenses that are related to your child's education.

Since a good deal of discipline is needed to resist spending money, you may prefer to accept less of a loan than could otherwise be borrowed. Before making this decision, consider the source and continuing availability of the loan. If you turn down part or all of a Federal Perkins Loan, which may offer the best deferment and cancellation provisions, the amount you decline will be offered to another needy student. If at a point later in the year you find that you really do need the Federal Perkins Loan, funds may no longer be available.

The FFEL and Direct Loan programs are not subject to the same limitations as the Federal Perkins Loan. In the case of the FFEL programs, unless the lender has a restriction on the number of applications it accepts from a student in a given year, you can borrow additional funds later as long as you show eligibility. Keep deadlines in mind since funds must normally be disbursed while your child is still enrolled. You and your child should weigh the temptation of spending available monies, your own propensity toward saving, and the source of the loan before deciding to turn it down or to delay applying for it.

SHOP FOR THE BEST DEAL

With the exception of ruling out higher-cost schools, you cannot control the level of tuition schools charge. The amount charged for tuition varies among schools and can also vary among programs of study within a school. Cost is not always an indicator of quality or prestige, so don't rule out lower-cost schools that also offer the programs of study in which your child is interested.

Most four-year programs include a certain level of liberal arts course work required for the degree; this course work does not directly affect the major. Your child may be able to take certain preparatory courses at a lower-cost school and then transfer to a higher-cost school for more advanced courses in the program of his or her choice. If the student intends to transfer to another school, he or she may well encounter a whole new set of deadlines and procedures. Different forms of aid might also be available, and the application process may differ significantly. Obtaining complete information well in advance of the time he or she actually transfers from one school to another is crucial in achieving a smooth transition.

Some states require a minimum length of residency in order to take advantage of in-state tuition.

Unlike private schools, public school tuition is usually affected by the state residency status of the student. Because they benefit from tax revenues, public colleges generally charge lower tuition, particularly to students who are residents of the state. Nonresident students at public schools are usually assessed a higher tuition rate. Distinguishing between resident and nonresident students at public colleges and universities appears to be a straightforward matter, but that distinction may be fairly complicated. Some states require a minimum length of residency in order to take advantage of in-state tuition. Students in the military assigned to a particular location, students who own property in another state or district, and international students who have resided in this country for a short time may discover that some schools or states will eye the bid for resident tuition rates with reservations. Questions on application forms about your addresses over a period of time, the state in which your child has a driver's license, and location of voter registration assist schools in determining residency status. Since the difference between resident and nonresident tuition can be hundreds or even thousands of dollars per year, seek clarification from schools under consideration.

CONSIDER COMMUNITY COLLEGE

Two-year colleges are usually funded in part by local or state taxes, so tuition is less expensive than at four-year colleges (about half the price of a public four-year college and 85 percent less than a private four-year college). A student can enroll at a community college for a year or two and take introductory and prerequisite courses at a significantly lower cost and then transfer to a four-year school to take courses in his or her major. Another way this will help you save money is in room and board costs since students can live at home and commute to local community colleges. Before enrolling in community college classes, get in touch with the four-year school that your child wants to attend because not all community college courses are transferable.

SHORTEN THE PROGRAM OF STUDY

Your child may be able to earn a degree or certificate in a shorter-than-normal period of time. For example, he or she might consider taking one extra course per term. Over a period of time, this can easily result in early graduation. Some schools do not charge more for enrolling in additional courses over and above the school's minimum definition of a full-time course load, while others charge by the credit hour. Even if there are additional charges for extra courses, ultimate savings on other expenses can be considerable.

Summer courses are another alternative. Taking summer classes can ease fall- and spring-semester class loads while still keeping you on track for early graduation. But, while financial aid may be available during summer school, you need to ascertain whether receiving aid during the summer reduces the amount of aid you can have for the rest of the year or program of study.

COLLEGE CREDIT BY EXAMINATION

Another approach your child can take to reduce costs is to earn credit by examination, thus reducing the amount of time required to receive a degree or certificate. Although you must pay an examination fee, the tests can offer cost-saving shortcuts to your child's educational destination.

> Become informed about the advantages of taking tests or classes for college credit while in high school. This can help save money later.

Be aware that schools differ in their treatment of credits earned through examination, so find out whether the school also charges a fee for establishing the credit on your child's academic record. It is also common for schools to prescribe a minimum number of credits that must be earned on campus if a student is to receive a degree from that school. Others simply limit the number of credits that can be earned by examination. If your child transfers, you may find that the new school does not accept credits granted by a previous school if they were earned in this manner. This can be particularly true if transferring from a two-year to a four-year college, since two-year colleges traditionally have a more liberal policy with respect to credit by examination.

Advanced Placement Program

The Advanced Placement (AP) program offers high school students the opportunity to complete college-level studies in subjects that range from biology to Spanish to English literature. At the conclusion of the AP class, students take a nationally administered exam in that subject area. If the student earns a high enough score, he or she may be able to earn college credit. Some students have been known to take so many AP exams that they have skipped their entire freshman year of college. The monetary value of potential AP credits is easy to determine. Consider the price of a year's worth of tuition and room and board. The more expensive a university is, the more money you will save if your child can skip a year through the AP program.

Colleges and universities set their own policies on the use of AP scores in granting appropriate placement or credit for entering freshmen. A list of participating colleges is available from the College Board Web site. However, specific questions about AP policies are best answered by officials at the college to which your child is applying for credit.

College-Level Examination Program (CLEP)

The College Board offers the College-Level Examination Program (CLEP). CLEP operates on the premise that college-level accomplishment can be gained not only in the classroom but also by independent study and experience.

There are two types of CLEP examinations: the General Examinations and the Subject Examinations. The General Examinations measure college-level achievement in five basic areas of the liberal arts: English composition, humanities, mathematics, natural sciences, and social sciences and history. These exams test material that is usually covered in the first two years of college and would normally be considered part of the general or liberal education requirement. The General Exami-

> If your child has pursued hobbies, talents, or interests to a high level of proficiency, you might consider turning that pursuit into college credit through the CLEP.

nations are not intended to measure specialized knowledge of a particular discipline, nor are they based on a particular curriculum or course of study. Rather, they are designed to evaluate broad-based ability that can be acquired in a number of ways, including through personal reading, employment, television, radio, adult classes, or advanced high school work.

The Subject Examinations measure a student's knowledge of subjects taught in specific college courses and are used to grant exemption from and credit for these courses. Thirty-four Subject Exams are offered in subjects that range from American government to macroeconomics and from English literature to information systems and computer applications. While there are no established curricula for subjects, texts and review books have been designed to help prepare for the tests.

Excelsior College Examinations

Your child can actually obtain an associate or baccalaureate degree in certain areas of concentration through Excelsior College of the University of the State of New York (formerly known as Regents College). The program (formerly known as the Proficiency Examination Program, or PEP) combines elements of proficiency testing, correspondence courses, life experiences, military courses, and actual college instruction in measuring progress toward a degree. The program assesses college-level knowledge and evaluates the number of credits your child has accumulated by a variety of acceptable methods. A degree is awarded when requirements have been fulfilled. Many schools also use the tests to perform their own evaluation of a student's college-level knowledge and award credit.

Excelsior College Examinations match the subject matter taught in standard college courses and measure knowledge in specific subjects. Four general areas of testing are:

➤ Arts and sciences

➤ Nursing

➤ Business

➤ Education

Credit can be given for introductory through upper-level knowledge, depending on the content of the test. The tests are developed and administered by Excelsior College and are given at Pearson Professional Centers throughout the United States and Canada. Detailed study guides are provided for each test. Each guide contains a content outline, bibliography, and sample questions.

Defense Activity for Non-Traditional Education Support (DANTES)

The DANTES program allows students to validate their grasp of knowledge and skills that would normally be acquired in college courses but have instead been acquired through independent self study and on-the-job and life experiences.

More than 1,900 colleges and universities in the United States award credit to students who receive high enough scores on more than 37 DANTES Subject Standardized Tests (DSST) in business, the humanities, social science, mathematics, physical science, and applied technology. The tests are administered primarily to current or previous members of the Armed Forces. Civilians may also take DSST exams, for a fee, year-round at colleges and universities throughout the United States and around the world. Before registering for an exam, check with your child's college or university to be sure that it will accept DSST credit for passing scores.

PAYMENT ALTERNATIVES

Once true costs have been determined and all resources have been researched and settled, options still remain to help you with your Expected Family Contribution (EFC). Most schools allow you to apply financial aid to school charges for tuition, fees, housing, meals, etc. If the aid has not actually been received, many schools allow you to defer payment until funds become available. If there is sufficient aid to cover all or most of the school's charges, the EFC is actually used for costs not directly charged by the school, such as books and supplies, transportation or commuting costs, and personal expenses. If your child commutes from home or lives off campus, expenses not owed to the school up front would include daily meals and perhaps monthly rent or mortgage.

PAYMENT PLANS

When very little or no financial aid is available, payment plans are usually available. These payment plans are either administered by the school itself or contracted to an outside agency, which charges a nominal fee. Payments typically begin a few months before the start of the school year and continue for the next twelve months or more. This is basically an installment plan, usually without interest charges. Such a plan may be preferable to taking a loan and may be just enough help to avoid the necessity of an Unsubsidized Federal Stafford, Direct Unsubsidized, or PLUS Loan. For more information, contact the school's business office.

ESTABLISH A HOME EQUITY LINE OF CREDIT

Many families pay some of their college expenses by borrowing against the equity in their home. Qualifying for a home equity line of credit is based on your credit and whether there is sufficient equity in your home. As opposed to a home equity loan, a home equity line of credit allows you to borrow when you need it, rather than all at once. In addition, home equity loans and lines of credit may be tax deductible, although you should always check with a tax adviser to be sure.

DO YOU QUALIFY FOR TAX CREDITS?

Hope Scholarship

The Hope Scholarship is actually a tax credit, not a scholarship. Tax credits are subtracted from the taxes you owe rather than reducing taxable income.

You must file a tax return and owe taxes to take advantage of it. The Hope tax credit is not refundable if you do not pay taxes or owe less in taxes than the maximum amount of the Hope tax credit for which you are eligible.

A family may claim a tax credit up to $1,650 per tax year per eligible student for the first two years of undergraduate study. You can claim up to 100 percent of the first $1,100 of your eligible education expenses and 50 percent of the next $1,100, for a maximum credit of $1,650. The actual amount of the credit depends on your income, the amount of qualified tuition and fees paid, and the amount of certain scholarships and allowances subtracted from tuition.

You are eligible for the maximum benefit with an adjusted gross income (AGI) of up to $55,000 for a single taxpayer or $110,000 for married taxpayers. The credit amount is phased out between $45,000 and $55,000 for single taxpayers and $90,000 and $110,000 for married taxpayers (2006 income limits). Your child must be enrolled at least half-time in an eligible program leading to a degree or certificate at an eligible school during the calendar year. To claim the Hope tax credit, you must complete IRS Form 8863.

The Lifetime Learning Tax Credit

Like the Hope Scholarship, the Lifetime Learning Tax Credit is available to individuals who file a tax return and owe taxes. This means the amount of the credit is subtracted from your actual tax liability. The Lifetime Learning Tax Credit is not refundable.

As a taxpayer, you can claim a tax credit up to $1,000 for all students in your family per tax year, per tax return. The credit is not limited to two years of study, like the Hope. You can claim up to 20 percent of the first $5,000 of eligible expenses for expenses paid after June 30, 2000, and prior to January 1, 2005, and up to 20 percent of $10,000 of eligible expenses for expenses paid after January 1, 2005.

The actual amount of the credit depends on your income, the amount of qualified tuition and fees paid, and the amount of certain scholarships and allowances subtracted from tuition. This credit is family based (e.g., $1,000 per family). You are eligible for the maximum benefit with an adjusted gross income (AGI) of up to $55,000 for a single taxpayer or $110,000 for married taxpayers. The credit amount is phased out between $45,000 and $55,000 for single taxpayers and $90,000 and $110,000 for married taxpayers (2006 income limits). Lifetime Learning Tax Credit is available for all years of postsecondary education and for courses to acquire or improve job skills, unlike the Hope credit which is only available for two years. To claim the Lifetime Learning Tax Credit, you must complete IRS Form 8863.

GET A JOB

If your child is looking for a job to help pay for his or her college tuition, he or she is not relegated to performing menial jobs, like scrubbing floors. There are a number of creative ways for your child to make some cash—the trick is knowing where to look.

Summer jobs, of course, are always an option for college students seeking cash. And they've come a long way since the days of flipping burgers and mowing lawns. Interesting job opportunities abound for enterprising young adults, including tour guide posts at national parks, amusement park ride operators, and lifeguards.

When hunting for work, teens should start by seeking out seasonal jobs. The National Park Service, for example, hires some 4,000 seasonal workers each summer to staff its nearly 400 parks across the country and in Guam, Puerto Rico, and the Virgin Islands. Many pay a small stipend of several hundred dollars per month with free room and board, making it more of an experience than a money-making venture. If your child is angling for a temporary gig at one of the more popular parks, including Yellowstone and the Grand Canyon, his or her application had better be competitive. Tens of thousands of would-be workers apply each year.

Cruise ships, too, provide an outlet for students over 18 who are looking for summer employment. But it's not all fun in the sun. Students should be prepared for physically demanding work, long hours, and low pay, insiders say. And they should come to the interview armed with energy to spare.

Don't forget amusement parks, which staff up during the summer months with teens who are 15 years and older, creating a camp-like atmosphere with low rent and on-site housing in many cases. Most need booth operators, licensed lifeguards, grounds assistants, security staff, concession stand help, and ride operators.

Finally, there's always lifeguarding, which pays well but requires certification in lifesaving and CPR, not to mention First Aid. Beach positions may be in demand, but apartment management companies tend to pay the most, offering Memorial Day to Labor Day employment to lifeguards at swimming pools throughout their apartment complexes.

Lifeguards can earn between $5,000 and $8,000 during the summer months, depending upon where they work. And pool operators, who are trained to manage a staff, operate the pumps, and control chemical levels in the pool, can make another $3,000 per summer. Note that many lifeguards work six days a week with no weekends off.

GET INVOLVED IN NATIONAL COMMUNITY SERVICE

The National and Community Service Trust Act of 1993 established the Corporation for National Service, which offers educational opportunities through service to American communities. Each state has a commission for national service through which participants are recruited and programs of service organized. The Corporation is the parent organization for the two AmeriCorps programs:

> ➤ AmeriCorps—National Civilian and Community Corps (NCCC)

> ➤ AmeriCorps—VISTA

AmeriCorps, a year-long national service program, offers college-age kids the chance to earn extra money and even college credit. Members of the program mentor at-risk youth, build affordable housing, provide health screenings, and help nonprofit groups nationwide.

AmeriCorps is the only U.S. service program of its kind, enrolling as many as 50,000 people a year. Its various programs have different requirements and deadlines. Some, like Teach for America, run on the school calendar and require a bachelor's degree. Others simply require applicants to be U.S. citizens over 17.

Beyond the benefits of serving a community in need, however, AmeriCorps members receive a $4,725 education award after a year of service, which can be used to pay tuition or repay student loans. They can earn up to two awards, meaning the program offers them an opportunity to put a dent of nearly $10,000 in their tuition bill.

While your child serves, he or she can apply for forbearance on student loans. That means no payments need to be made during that time. Interest continues to accumulate, but if your child qualifies for forbearance and completes his or her term of service, AmeriCorps pays some or all of the interest that accrued on those loans.

AmeriCorps members may be able to cut higher education bills even further. Some colleges offer course credit or scholarships for participation in the program. The nonprofit has convinced many schools to offer incentives to AmeriCorps members, whether it's by matching the education award, offering a scholarship, or granting course credit for experiential learning to AmeriCorps alums.

WHAT ABOUT MILITARY SERVICE?

The military offers several ways your child can reach his or her educational goals. Military educational programs benefit men and women who serve in the country's defense forces. Participants can receive an education while serving in the military or serve in the military first and then concentrate on postsecondary education. Some programs offer only one of these options while others combine them.

Educational Benefits for Veterans

The current version of veterans benefits is applicable to individuals who have entered the Army, Navy, Air Force, Marines, or Coast Guard on or after June 30, 1985. Authorized under the Montgomery G.I. Bill, the program differs based on whether the student is on active duty or in the Reserves.

Benefits for Active Duty

Active duty benefits can be used for the purpose of obtaining a college education while on active duty, after serving at least three years, and can be redeemed after separation from the service. In order to be eligible, your child must have a high school diploma or its equivalent before completing the required period of active duty. The serviceperson contributes $100 per month in the form of pay reduction for the first twelve months of active duty. If your child separates from the service, he or she must have received an honorable discharge and must have served either continuously on active duty for three years or for two years followed by four years in the Selected Reserves. Benefits must be used within ten years of discharge.

Benefits for Selected Reserve Duty

While in the Selected Reserves (Army Reserve, Navy Reserve, Air Force Reserve, Marine Corps Reserve, Coast Guard Reserve, Army National Guard, and Air National Guard), your child can take advantage of educational benefits authorized under the Montgomery G.I. Bill. The service commitment must be for at least six years, and certain eligibility requirements must be met, including having a high school diploma or its equivalent. Your child will not be eligible if he or she already has a bachelor's degree. These benefits are available only during the period of your child's participation in the Selected Reserves. Benefits are payable for up to thirty-six months. For more information on veterans educational benefits, go to www.gibill.va.gov.

Community College of the Air Force (CCAF)/Servicemember Opportunity College (SOC)

Enlisted personnel can also receive degrees through the Community College of the Air Force (CCAF) or the Servicemember Opportunity College (SOC) of the Army, Navy, Marines, or Coast Guard. These networks enable enlisted men and women to pursue a traditional degree through arrangements with a number of colleges. Participating schools offer flexible academic programs that take into account the lifestyles of servicemembers, with their time constraints and pattern of frequent reassignments.

To take advantage of one of these opportunities, the serviceperson must be stationed at a base near a college campus that has provided the necessary scheduling for off-duty military personnel. Each base has an education officer who can assist your child if he or she wants to enroll in a local college or take correspondence courses.

Tuition assistance is available in the form of tuition discounts for servicemembers and their families pursuing their education through this network. Your child can take advantage of this program while in the service and still receive benefits under the G.I. Bill when he or she gets out. Servicemembers and their families can enroll in associate, bachelor, and graduate degree programs through SOC.

Tuition Assistance Program

The Armed Forces offers military personnel up to 100 percent tuition assistance for college courses taken during off-duty hours. Armed Forces Tuition Assistance (TA) is a benefit paid to eligible members of the Army, Navy, Marines, Air Force, and Coast Guard. Through Congress, each service branch has the ability to pay up to 100 percent for the tuition expenses of its members. Each service branch has its own criteria for eligibility, obligated service, application processes, and restrictions. This money is usually paid directly to the institution by the individual service branch.

There are other options available to military personnel to help them pay for college, including tuition-free college courses offered by the Navy to personnel on sea duty and credit offered by some institutions for military experience, such as the U.S. Coast Guard Institute. For more information, students and counselors should contact their local military recruiting office.

CHAPTER.

8

Crack the Code: What Deal Did You Really Get?

FAST FACTS

➤ **Find out how much college "really" costs.** College costs can vary widely. If your child attends a local community college and lives at home, your out-of-pocket costs for the entire academic year may only be a few thousand dollars. A state-supported public university will have a total cost of education anywhere from $10,000 to $20,000 a year. An Ivy League college education can easily cost $45,000 annually.

➤ **If you were denied assistance when your first child started college, reapply for financial aid for your second attendee.** The results of the need analysis calculations are substantially different when you have two or more children in college compared to only one child in college.

➤ **Compare the different packaging philosophies and awarding criteria at each school you are considering.** If your child has been accepted at many institutions and has received many different financial aid packages, compare the packages. Calculate what the out-of-pocket costs will be, how much of the award package will be in grants or scholarships versus loans, and what is the expected renewability of scholarships and grants.

PACKAGING

Once your child's eligibility for financial aid has been established, the next step is to develop a financial aid award. The process of combining different types of aid from a variety of sources to meet your need is called packaging. It fills the gap between the cost of attending a particular school and the amount you can afford to draw from your own income and assets to pay those costs. Packaging is the way financial aid administrators seek to distribute limited resources equitably. It is important to understand that the FAFSA processor does not determine your financial need or your financial aid package. The individual schools make these decisions, and they do so by taking into account the Cost of Attendance (COA), your Expected Family Contribution (EFC) and other resources, the amount of financial aid funds available, the number of students requesting assistance, and the goals established by the school.

For schools that package based on application deadlines, there is frequently an earlier deadline for first-year students than there is for returning students. First-year applicants must be aware of the timing of admissions notifications and when they can expect to receive notification of the financial assistance. These two pieces of information are extremely important, as in many cases, the decision to attend a particular school cannot be made until you know how much financial assistance will be extended. For example, if the aid application deadline is March 15, award notifications might be sent by April 1. The school might have a reply date of May 1, by which time you must notify the school whether your child plans to attend that school (and perhaps submit a deposit to hold a place in the incoming class). Your child may have been notified of his or her acceptance for admission to the school in January but did not have a financial aid offer

> The first resource considered in the packaging process is the EFC. If the EFC is equal to or greater than the COA, a school may award your child merit-based aid of its own, or you have the option of borrowing a Federal Unsubsidized Stafford Loan or Direct Unsubsidized Loan.

until April. Since you may be weighing admission offers from several schools, packaging becomes a means of tipping the scales for some schools.

Before packaging can begin, the aid administrator must have the results of your FAFSA. It is your responsibility to ensure that the FAFSA is submitted to the FAFSA processor in time to meet school deadlines.

It is not uncommon for schools to have their own institutional aid applications; nor is it unusual for schools to require tax returns or other documents to verify or further explain data reported on the FAFSA. The federal government also requires some financial aid applicants to verify the income information reported on the FAFSA by submitting tax returns to the school's financial aid office.

It is a good idea to complete your income tax return as early as possible. This ensures that if the school or the government requires a tax return, you can promptly submit it to the school and avoid unnecessary delays in award notification.

If you were not required to file a tax return, you may be asked to provide other forms of documentation. All types of income summaries, such as W-2 forms, Social Security statements, and welfare receipts, should be kept accessible in the event they are requested by the school.

COST OF ATTENDANCE

To understand the packaging process, you must understand the concepts leading to it. We have already defined need, and we have reviewed in detail one of the components of the need equation: the EFC. The remaining component is the Cost of Attendance (COA).

Cost of Attendance is frequently referred to as the student budget, and it takes into consideration expenses that are related to your child's education. These education costs include:

➤ Tuition and fees

➤ Room

➤ Board

➤ Books and supplies

➤ Transportation

➤ Personal expenses

Costs also include other types of expenses, such as loan fees, expenses related to a disability (if they are necessary for attendance and are not already covered by other assisting agencies), costs related to a study-abroad program, and costs related to a cooperative education work experience.

Your child is expected to live on a reasonable but modest budget while attending college. Most schools use standard budgets that reflect the average amount a student spends for each budget category. For example, rather than calculating individual budgets for each student based on their major, schools usually use an average amount for a broad category of students. Your child's actual costs may vary slightly from the standard budget, but aid is normally based on the averages. If there is some documentable reason that your son or daughter will incur costs greater than the average, be sure the aid administrator is made aware of them in order to adjust the package.

The COA varies by type of institution and the costs associated with attending that institution. For example, independent (or private) colleges and universities do not receive operating subsidies from the government and therefore must charge students higher tuitions and fees than a state-supported community college or other public institution of higher learning. Consequently, the Cost of Attendance at a private college or university is usually higher than that of a public college or university. The COA can also vary by individual student. A student who lives off campus may have a higher room and board cost than a student who is living in a residence hall.

Although the COA varies by institution and student, the EFC should remain relatively constant no matter which college your child decides to attend. Thus, need varies because costs vary. This is an important concept to keep in mind when helping your child decide which institution to attend.

Tuition and Fees

The tuition and fee component of your child's Cost of Attendance is fairly straightforward. Tuition and fees are the actual amount you are charged rather than an average based on a group of students. Depending upon the type of program your child is enrolled in, other charges, such as laboratory fees and equipment costs, may also be included in this category.

Room

Room includes housing costs incurred by your child. The nature of the room expense varies greatly according to the student's circumstances, depending on whether he or she lives on campus, off campus, or at home with you.

Board

Like the room expense, board is an allowance that varies according to the student's place of residence and other factors. This allowance normally provides for reasonable costs necessary to provide nutritionally adequate meals for the single student.

Transportation

For students who commute to and from campus, the transportation allowance includes the cost of getting to and from school each class day. The transportation allowance is not intended to cover the cost of purchasing a car, but it may be sufficient for parking and general maintenance of a car. The allowance is not usually adequate to pay for insurance coverage. If your child attends a school in an area where public transportation is adequate and reliable, the transportation allowance is usually based on the use of that system.

Personal Expenses

Student budgets also allow for miscellaneous personal expenses. Everyday necessities, such as personal hygiene and laundry expenses, are included in this cost category, as is a modest clothing allowance. Many schools provide a small budget for an occasional movie or other form of entertainment.

CALCULATING NEED FOR NEED-BASED AID

Once the school has established reasonable standard student aid budgets and the most appropriate one is selected for a particular student, the packaging process can begin. The basic principle is that the student has the first obligation to pay for education costs.

As discussed earlier, the difference between the Cost of Attendance at a particular school and your ability to contribute toward those costs establishes your need for certain types of financial assistance, generally referred to as need-based aid. Again, here is the formula for need-based aid:

Cost of Attendance (COA)

– Expected Family Contribution (EFC)

= Need

If your child has been awarded other types of assistance, such as an academic scholarship from a community organization, these resources must be taken into account when you are packaged with need-based assistance. With this in mind, here is the formula used when there are other resources to take into account:

Cost of Attendance (COA)

– Expected Family Contribution (EFC) and other resources

= Need

Before awarding any form of student assistance, the school must first determine whether you are eligible for a Federal Pell Grant. The Federal Pell Grant is considered the foundation of the aid package. All other assistance is built around this grant. The aid administrator must calculate the actual amount of the Federal Pell Grant award based upon your EFC, Cost of Attendance for an academic year, length of your child's period of enrollment, and his or her enrollment status.

Once eligibility for a Federal Pell Grant has been considered, the school determines whether the student will receive assistance from external sources. This type of assistance includes any state grant or scholarship, private scholarships (such as service club awards and merit scholarships), and any student educational assistance benefits such as veterans educational benefits. When all of your educational resources have been subtracted from your Cost of Attendance along with the EFC, any remaining need for student assistance is met with a combination of resources over which the school has control, based on the school's packaging policies and philosophy.

NON-NEED AID ELIGIBILITY

The amount you may receive from the non-need-based federal programs (such as Federal Unsubsidized Stafford Loan and Direct Unsubsidized Loan) is determined somewhat differently from the other federal programs. As discussed earlier, the EFC is not considered when your eligibility for non-need-based assistance is determined. However, the amount that may be borrowed is limited to the difference between the Cost of Attendance at a particular institution and the estimated amount of other assistance you receive. The formula for non-need-based federal financial aid is:

Cost of Attendance

− Estimated Financial Assistance

= Need

It should now be clear that the amount of aid you receive is directly related to the Cost of Attendance at schools. The EFC should be constant from school to school, unless your EFC is adjusted based on individual unusual circumstances by the aid administrator at one school but not at another.

If your child applies to two schools (one high-cost and the other low-cost), it is quite possible that the amount of aid offered by the high-cost school will be enough to cover the difference in costs between the two. By offering more aid, the actual cost to you is the same regardless of which school the student actually attends. When this occurs, one of the fundamental purposes of student aid is accomplished: to provide access and choice. You may incur a heavier debt burden or your child may be required to work more hours at one school versus another. You may decide that it is worthwhile to assume this additional responsibility if it means your child will be able to attend the school of his or her choice.

WHAT'S IN THE AID PACKAGE

To put the pieces of the financial aid puzzle together to form a complete picture, you need to know what you can expect to receive in response to your applications for aid, as well as what you must do once an offer of assistance has been extended.

Because there are many potential sources of aid, to secure funding you must usually complete and submit numerous forms and documents. Not surprisingly, you can expect to receive a great deal of paper or numerous electronic messages in response. Anticipate receiving some or all of the following types of responses from application processors and schools:

➤ Student Aid Report (SAR) or SAR Information Acknowledgment from the Central Processing System (CPS)

➤ Notification of aid from a state agency regarding eligibility for a state scholarship, grant, or some other form of state assistance

➤ Notification of aid from private sources, if applicable

➤ Preliminary estimate from the school of the amounts and types of aid for which you may be eligible

➤ If necessary, a letter from the school requesting additional documents, such as an institutional application, tax returns, and other documents required for verification

➤ Financial aid notification (award letter) from the school

➤ Loan applications or promissory notes

Notification of State Aid

To be considered for a state award, some states may require you to file documents in addition to the FAFSA. The information that state agencies receive contains your financial information as well as a calculation of your EFC. In most cases, state agencies use this information to determine eligibility for state assistance; others award state aid via the school's aid administrator in compliance with state guidelines.

State aid is often channeled directly to your child's school and is always considered as an available resource when your award package is constructed. Pay particular attention to the terms and conditions of state aid, as it may be restricted to use in-state, to specific components of the Cost of Attendance (such as tuition and fees only), or, in the case of special awards, to particular majors. If your child has been offered state assistance, he or she will have to return a signed acceptance of the state award by a specified deadline. Again, any published deadline should be taken with the utmost seriousness; failure to reply by a specified date may result in the award being canceled, and except in extraordinary circumstances, the state aid is not reinstated.

Many states notify the school that you have been awarded state assistance. However, because this practice is not uniform, it is wise to notify your child's intended schools directly that he or she is the recipient of a state award. Schools can then take the state award into account when constructing your financial aid package. Otherwise, you might find out what impact the state award has on your package only after your child has enrolled.

Notification of Aid from Private Sources

The award notification techniques of private aid sources vary in style and timing. In some cases, you receive some type of acknowledgment, whether or not you actually receive any money. In others, only successful applicants are contacted. Some organizations notify you in the spring that you have won an award, others notify you in the summer, and sometimes you are not notified until the fall term.

Should you receive funding from a source outside of the school, it is crucial that you inform the financial aid office immediately. Failure to do so can result in your having to repay all or part of the aid received from the school and can jeopardize future aid eligibility.

Preliminary Estimates

The following sample financial aid packages illustrate how aid may be combined in different ways and in accordance with differing packaging philosophies to meet your needs. Keep in mind that these are only examples; the actual financial aid packages offered by your school will almost certainly be different. When reviewing the sample packages, it is important to note that they embody the following important points:

> ➤ The Cost of Attendance will vary significantly according to school type (e.g., public versus private, two-year versus four-year).

> ➤ The amounts and sources of aid will vary by school.

> ➤ The single constant in the various aid packages is the EFC.

Community College Aid Package (full-time, first-year student)	
Budget	$5,000
Expected Family Contribution	–2,000
Need	$3,000
Federal Pell Grant	1,175
State Grant	500
Federal Perkins Loan	500
Federal Stafford Loan	– 825
Unmet Need	$0

In this example, the Cost of Attendance at the community college is relatively low. The student's financial need is completely met through grants and loans.

Public University Aid Package (full-time, first-year student)	
Budget	$12,000
Expected Family Contribution	–2,000
Need	$10,000
Federal Pell Grant	1,175
State Grant	1,000
Federal Perkins Loan	1,000
Federal Work-Study	2,000
Federal Stafford Loan	–3,500
Unmet Need	$1,325

In this example, the cost of attending a public state school is greater than the cost of the community college, primarily because the fees are higher. Note that the Expected Family Contribution (EFC) is the same as at the community college example.

Although cost is a factor in calculating Federal Pell Grants because of the way in which Pell Grant awards are determined, the student's Federal Pell Grant amount remains the same. Since tuition and fees are higher at a state university than they are at a community college, this student is eligible for a larger state grant.

The state university in this example has included a Federal Stafford Loan of $3,500 in the package. This was done so that more of the student's need could be met. If the student decides to accept this loan, he or she will have to complete and submit a loan application for the Federal Stafford Loan. If the student declines this loan, the school may not be willing or able to replace it with another form of aid. Instead, the student will have to come up with this money on his or her own, possibly through employment or from personal savings.

Private University Aid Package (full-time, first-year student)	
Budget	$24,000
Expected Family Contribution	−2,000
Need	$22,000
Federal Pell Grant	1,175
State Grant	2,500
Outside Scholarship	3,000
Institutional Grant	7,825
Federal Perkins Loan	2,000
Direct Stafford Loan	3,500
Federal Work-Study	−2,000
Unmet Need	$0

In this example, the Cost of Attendance is considerably greater than in the previous two examples. Again, because the tuition and fees are higher, this student is eligible for a larger state grant than he or she would have received at either the community college or state university. The aid offered also includes a Direct Stafford Loan for $3,500. Because this student has a large amount of need, he or she has been offered an institutional grant of $7,825.

Institutional Financial Aid Award Letters

Most schools send a document known as an Award Letter, a Notification of Financial Assistance, or an Offer Letter. We will refer to any type of award notification as an Award Letter.

An Award Letter describes the sources, types, and amounts of financial aid being offered and is a type of commitment or contract between your child and the school. Take the terms and conditions of the award seriously and do nothing to jeopardize the assistance. This includes carefully and thoroughly reading the information enclosed with the Award Letter and responding to all required deadlines. Because financial aid resources are limited, schools often cancel awards made to students who fail to return forms on time. This aid is then reoffered to other needy and eligible students. While aid administrators work diligently to ensure that as many deserving students as possible receive assistance, they cannot extend aid offers indefinitely. You must accept the responsibility of keeping in contact with the school or risk losing the aid that has been offered to you.

Make sure your Federal Pell Grant is listed correctly. A "0" Expected Family Contribution should give you a maximum Pell Grant of $4,310 per award year.

Award Letters from individual schools differ in style and format, but the same basic information is generally provided. Ideally, the Award Letter, and any accompanying materials, provide specific and easy-to-understand information about:

➤ Your Cost of Attendance

➤ Your need for assistance and how that need was determined

➤ A listing of the types of aid being offered to meet your need

➤ When the aid will be disbursed: before, on, or after the start of classes; periodically during the term; by semester, trimester, quarter; or some other frequency, depending on the school's academic calendar

➤ How the aid will be disbursed (by crediting the student account or by cash payment to you)

➤ Any conditions of the offer, such as academic requirements, minimum course load, or satisfactory academic progress

Schools may require you to accept or decline the types of aid being offered and sign and return the Award Letter to the financial aid office. However, more and more schools are only requiring a response if you wish to change the aid package offer. If a loan has been offered, you also have to sign additional forms, such as a promissory note.

Reading Between the Lines

Imagine this scenario. Your combined family income is less than $30,000 per year. Your child plans to enroll in a five-year physical therapy program at a private college in Pennsylvania. You receive the Award Letter from the school but toss it aside because the financial aid lingo is making your head spin. After all, the guidance counselor told you that you'd probably get enough grant money to pay for your child's education because of your low family income. But wait. If you took the time to analyze the Award Letter, you might find some surprises. For example, you might find that your child's school of choice is only covering 80 percent of the total Cost of Attendance. Do you think this is a worst-case scenario that won't happen to your family? Think again. It happens to college-bound students all the time.

We're not trying to scare you. Rather, we're trying to show you how important those Award Letters are, what you need to know in order to fully understand what they mean, and how to compare them across institutions.

To help you analyze and compare Award Letters, we have constructed three Award Letters from three different schools. Each of these Award Letters is similar to what you can expect to receive in the mail during the financial aid process. By using the information contained in these Letters, we will show you how to compare Award Letters based on a proven seven-step process. By following the steps outlined here, you will be able to compare all types of Award Letters and determine how much aid you're really getting.

UNIVERSITY OF LEARNING
FINANCIAL AID AWARD NOTIFICATION
2008–09

Date: 04/29/08

ID#: 000000009

Dear Student:

We are pleased to inform you that you are eligible to receive the financial assistance indicated in the area labeled "Your Financial Aid" for the 2008–09 academic year. We estimated your budget based on the following assumptions:

Non-resident and living on campus.

	FALL	SPRING	TOTAL
Tuition and Fees	$3,849	$3,849	$7,698
Room and Board	3,769	3,770	7,539
Books	420	420	840
Transportation	973	974	1,947
Personal Expenses	369	369	738
Estimated Cost of Attendance	**$9,380**	**$9,382**	**$18,762**

If you have any questions, please contact us. If you know that you will be receiving any financial aid from sources not listed on your Financial Aid Award Letter, you must report each additional resource and the amount to the Office of Student Financial Aid. This award is based on information that you have supplied. If any of the information you submitted is incorrect or has changed, your awards may be adjusted.

Your Financial Aid

	FALL	SPRING	TOTAL
Federal Pell Grant	$1,950	$1,950	$3,900
Federal Direct Subsidized Loan	1,750	1,750	3,500
Institutional Grant	432	432	864
Total Financial Aid	**4,132**	**4,132**	**8,264**
Unmet Need	**$5,248**	**$5,240**	**$10,488**

UNIVERSITY OF THE U.S.
FINANCIAL AID AWARD NOTIFICATION
2008–09

Date: 04/29/08
ID#: 000000008

Dear Student:

We are pleased to inform you that you are eligible to receive the financial assistance indicated in the area labeled "Your Financial Aid" for the 2008–09 academic year. We estimated your budget based on the following assumptions:

Non-resident and living on campus.

	FALL	SPRING	TOTAL
Tuition and Fees	$9,502	$9,503	$19,005
Room and Board	2,835	2,835	5,670
Books	410	410	820
Transportation	875	875	1,750
Personal Expenses	378	377	755
Estimated Cost of Attendance	**$14,000**	**$14,000**	**$28,000**

If you have any questions, please contact us. If you know that you will be receiving any financial aid from sources not listed on your Financial Aid Award Letter, you must report each additional resource and the amount to the Office of Student Financial Aid. This award is based on information that you have supplied. If any of the information you submitted is incorrect or has changed, your awards may be adjusted.

Your Financial Aid

	FALL	SPRING	TOTAL
Federal Pell Grant	$1,450	$1,450	$2,900
Federal SEOG Grant	725	725	1,450
Institutional Grant	500	500	1,000
Federal Work-Study	1,250	1,250	2,500
Federal Perkins Loan	1,250	1,250	2,500
Subsidized Stafford Loan	1,750	1,750	3,500
Unsubsidized Stafford Loan	2,000	2,000	4,000
Total Financial Aid	**$8,925**	**$8,925**	**$17,850**
Unmet Need	**$5,075**	**$5,075**	**$10,150**

UNIVERSITY OF PETERSON
FINANCIAL AID AWARD NOTIFICATION
2008–09

Date: 04/29/08
ID#: 000000007

Dear Student:

We are pleased to inform you that you are eligible to receive the financial assistance indicated in the area labeled "Your Financial Aid" for the 2008–09 academic year. We estimated your budget based on the following assumptions:

Non-resident and living on campus.

	FALL	SPRING	TOTAL
Tuition and Fees	$14,955	$14,955	$29,910
Room and Board	4,194	4,193	8,387
Books	450	450	900
Transportation	350	350	700
Personal Expenses	1,295	1,293	2,588
Estimated Cost of Attendance	**$21,244**	**$21,241**	**$42,485**

If you have any questions, please contact us. If you know that you will be receiving any financial aid from sources not listed on this Financial Aid Award Letter, you must report each additional resource and the amount to the Office of Student Financial Aid. This award is based on information that you have supplied. If any of the information you submitted is incorrect or has changed, your awards may be adjusted.

Your Financial Aid

	FALL	SPRING	TOTAL
Institutional Grant	$10,730	$10,730	$21,460
Federal Pell Grant	2,155	2,155	4,310
Federal SEOG Grant	2,000	2,000	4,000
Federal Work-Study	1,713	1,712	3,425
Total Financial Aid	**$16,598**	**$16,597**	**$33,195**
Unmet Need	**$4,646**	**$4,644**	**$9,290**

SEVEN-STEP PROCESS FOR COMPARING AWARD LETTERS

1. **Create a spreadsheet.** The best way to analyze your awards is to create a spreadsheet that contains the following information:

	U. of Learning	U. of the U.S.	U. of Peterson
Cost of Attendance	$18,762	$28,000	$42,485
Tuition and Fees	7,698	19,005	29,910
Room and Board	7,539	5,670	8,387
Books	840	820	900
Transportation	1,947	1,750	700
Personal Expenses	738	755	2,558
Grants and Scholarships	4,764	5,350	29,510
Loans	3,500	10,000	0
Work-Study	0	2,500	3,425
Expected Family Contribution	9,550	9,550	9,550
Balance	$948	$600	$0

2. **Calculate your cost of attendance.** Financial Aid Award Letters should provide you with a Cost of Attendance (COA) budget that includes all projected costs, including tuition and fees, room and board, books, transportation, personal expenses, etc. If your Award Letter doesn't provide all this information, call the school's financial aid office to get an estimate of the total yearly budget. This information is critical to understanding exactly how much you will need for the academic year.

3. **Add up your grants and scholarships.** Your Financial Aid Award Letters break down the exact amount of aid you will be receiving from various sources. Go through the list and note any grants or scholarships. It's important to note what part of your aid package comes in the form of grants and scholarships because these awards (gift aid) do not have to be paid back. Enter the amount of the gift aid you will receive from each college on your spreadsheet. For example, if your Award Letter states that you will receive $4,764 in grants and scholarships, as is the case with the University of Learning, enter that amount in the "Grants and Scholarships" field.

4. **Add up your loans.** You may have been approved for one or several different types of loans. For now, add up the amount of money that you are being offered in loans and enter that amount in the appropriate field on your spreadsheet. For example, the University of the U.S. is awarding $10,000 in loans. Enter that amount in the "Loans" field. If you decide to borrow, make conservative but realistic estimates of the amount you actually need. The best advice is to borrow only what is needed. Also, keep track of the amounts you borrow, from whom you borrowed, and when the loan or loans become payable. This is essential information for avoiding loan default.

5. **Calculate your work-study aid.** Each school will provide an amount they expect your child to contribute to his or her education through work. For example, the University of Peterson is offering $3,425 in work-study aid. Enter the amount in the "Work-Study" field.

6. **Enter your expected family contribution (EFC).** This figure is determined from the Federal Methodology based on information you submitted on your FAFSA. In all three cases, your EFC is $9,550. Enter that amount in the "Expected Family Contribution" field.

7. **Calculate the gap.** Now find the sum of scholarships and grants, loans, Work-Study, and your EFC and subtract that number from the Cost of Attendance. Is there a balance, or "gap," between the amount you're receiving in aid and your yearly budget? If so, enter that amount in the "Balance" field for each school.

Interpreting the Numbers

Here are some things to consider when analyzing the numbers in your Financial Aid Award spreadsheet:

> **How much is your balance or "gap"?** If you're lucky, you won't have a balance for any of your colleges. But don't panic if you do. Determine which school has the highest gap. In this case, it is the

University of Learning. Notice that it has the lowest Cost of Attendance but the highest gap. This is important to remember when interpreting the numbers in a Financial Aid Award Letter. It's not the original Cost of Attendance but the final "sticker price" that matters.

Now that you know which college will cost the most, ask yourself, "Is there a way to find money to cover the gap?" There are a number of ways, including paying more than the EFC figure in the Award Letter, increasing student borrowing, working more hours, and taking out a PLUS Loan.

➤ **Look again at your loans and scholarships.** Your best financial deal probably contains more money in scholarships and less money in loan dollars. Based on expected freshman-year borrowing, determine your debt burden once your child graduates. Determine this amount for each institution. You have to multiply the amount of your loan(s) by four or five years, depending on how long it will take for your child to graduate. In addition, you should take into account that you will have to borrow even more as the Cost of Attendance increases each year. Answer the following questions to determine the best loan deal:

- What are the terms of your loans?

- What are the interest rates?

- Do you pay the yearly interest rate while your child is enrolled, or is it covered by the government?

- Is any money due while your child is enrolled, or is it deferred until after graduation?

➤ **What are the terms of the scholarships and grants?** Some schools award scholarships and grants for the first year of study only. Find out if this gift aid is good for all four years and whether or not it will increase as tuition increases over the course of your child's study. If the aid is good only for one year, then under what conditions will your child be able to receive assistance in future years? Also, if the scholarship is merit-based, find out if there is a minimum grade point average your child must maintain and whether or not your child can keep the scholarship if he or she changes majors.

➤ **Are you willing to have your child participate in a work-study program?** You need to figure out how much time your child will actually be able to devote to work. How many hours per week will be necessary for him or her to make the amount that is listed on the Award Letter? Can your child work the necessary hours and still have time to study and participate in extracurricular activities? If not, you might want to ask the aid office if it would be willing to convert at least some of the work-study dollars into loan dollars.

➤ **How is the financial aid package adjusted based on tuition increases?** Let's face it, tuition is not going to remain constant. Check with the financial aid office to find out what its policy is for renewing an aid package from one year to the next. For example, ask: "If tuition increases by 5 percent in each of the next three years and my EFC remains the same, what will happen to the awarded scholarships, grants, and loans?" The answer to this question will give you an idea of what to expect past your child's first year of college.

➤ **Ask questions.** If there is something on the Financial Aid Award Letter that you don't understand, pick up the phone and call the financial aid counselor at the school. He or she will be able to answer any questions you might have about the Award Letter.

To determine which schools are offering the best aid packages, look at your loan amounts. You can figure out how much will be owed at each school after your child graduates to get a clear picture of what your financial situation will be like once college is over. However, you shouldn't simply pick the school offering the lowest loan amounts, unless cost is your only concern. Remember, a high-quality education should not be based solely on the sticker price of a school. Base the final decision on which school can provide your child with the best academic, social, and financial environment.

In this particular case, the University of Peterson meets your entire need without awarding anything in loan dollars. This is the type of deal you should look for.

EVALUATING AID PACKAGES

Once the educational aspects of the decision-making process have been considered, other factors should become part of your evaluation of financial aid offers. Be aware that the largest financial aid package is not always the best. Because of differences in Cost of Attendance between the various types of schools, the largest offer in terms of dollars can also be the one with the greatest gap between cost and available resources. If that gap cannot be filled by some other source, the largest offer may not be enough for your child to attend that school.

Even two offers that fully meet your need may not be equal. If the estimated expense budget used to calculate your need is unrealistically low, you may have more real unmet need than the Award Letter suggests. Compare the stated costs with those of similar schools to verify the reasonableness of a school's estimated Cost of Attendance figures.

Packages containing equal dollars and similar unmet need are not always the same either. There may be a higher proportion of gift aid and, consequently, a smaller loan and work obligation. Or, one package may offer a higher proportion in self-help aid and less grant aid. Similarly, not all scholarships are the same. Some are automatically renewable; others are renewable only under certain conditions, such as continued high academic performance. Some are nonrenewable and good for the first year only. So a $500 scholarship that is renewable might actually be better than a $1,000 scholarship with many conditions associated with it or a $1,500 nonrenewable one.

Ask how $3,000 in outside aid would change your aid package. You can use any amount when you ask this question, but use the same amount at each school. That way you will get consistent answers about how outside aid might affect your package.

For some students, certain types of packages are better than others. If your child plans to enter a low-paying profession or faces graduate or professional training before entering the job market, you should look more cautiously at substantial loan obligations. Equal loan amounts do not necessarily equate to the same level of obligation. While the terms and conditions of the specific federal loan programs are the same from school to school, there are variations among the types of federal loan programs offered. Higher interest rates, fewer deferment options, earlier payback requirements, and higher minimum payments can make one loan more costly than another, even when the same amount is borrowed.

Because of limited funding, the extra cost of out-of-state tuition may not be met in full at public colleges, making this choice costly for the family. In contrast, most private colleges meet full need and do not leave a gap. Therefore, when wishing to attend out-of-state colleges, in the majority of cases it may be cheaper to attend a high-cost private versus a low-cost out-of-state public institution.

When evaluating loans, it is helpful to understand the terms and conditions of each program. While Federal Perkins, Federal Stafford, and Direct Loan programs have relatively low interest rates, the Federal Perkins Loan has different deferments and more cancellation provisions than the Federal Stafford and Direct Loans. Remember, since they can have a significant impact upon your child's postgraduate activities and the quality of his or her life after graduation, loans deserve a great deal of your attention during the evaluation process.

In assessing aid packages, bear in mind that loans must be repaid regardless of whether or not your child completes his or her program of study. Dropping out of school or not being able to find a job in a chosen career does not relieve the obligation to repay an education loan.

The bottom line? Calculate what the out-of-pocket costs will be, how much of the award package will be in grants or scholarships versus loans, and particularly, what is the expected renewability of scholarships and grants. If there is a large discrepancy in offers among your selected schools, go back to the information you collected about each school; perhaps one offer seems to be merit-based but actually is based on need. Finally, you must balance the value of the award package with the education your child will receive.

CHANGES TO THE AID PACKAGE

While packaging policies affect the amounts and types of aid initially offered, they also influence the ways in which adjustments are made to your award when circumstances change. Most often, adjustments are made to an aid package because the resources available to you have changed. For instance, if your child receives additional private grant funds from an outside organization after a package has been developed and offered, the aid administrator must review that package to see if it is still valid. Since federal regulations limit the amount of aid students can receive and because institutional aid is limited, financial aid administrators are usually required to reexamine eligibility for assistance when they become aware that additional resources are available.

> Be proactive! Contact the financial aid office at your selected college to make sure your file is complete and no documents are missing. Check and double-check on a regular basis.

The school determines the manner in which a financial aid package is adjusted. If the outside source of funding is in the form of a grant, the school's policy may be to reduce grant aid already offered. The school may have a policy to replace loans with outside resources in order to reduce the total debt burden. If a student's full need has not been previously met, the school might have a policy that allows outside resources to replace unmet need before affecting aid already offered. The need of other students and the extent of available funding for each type of aid program ultimately influence the way packages are adjusted.

You are obligated to notify schools of any additional resources received even after the school has extended an aid offer. If your child has been given a scholarship by a local community organization, her eligibility for aid will probably be affected. In most cases, all forms of resources available to the student, whether they are coming from the parents or from a scholarship that a student has secured from an outside agency, are taken under consideration in any need-based financial aid award. Request that if a reduction in aid is required, it be taken from loan awards.

To comply with federal requirements, schools must ensure that financial aid applicants do not receive more federal aid than permitted. If you are receiving non-need-based assistance, such as an Unsubsidized Federal Stafford Loan or Direct Unsubsidized Loan or a scholarship, the total aid received cannot exceed the Cost of Attendance. If the financial aid administrator becomes aware of an educational expense not already covered by the standard student budget, the Cost of Attendance may be increased so the additional resources pay for that expense rather than decreasing the aid offered. Similarly, the EFC may be adjusted to avoid an over-award if there are extenuating circumstances.

If you have special circumstances you want the aid office to know about, send them a letter apart from your application. Financial aid is about numbers, so if there are extra expenses you want to have considered, be sure to give the figures—fewer words and more figures are good! Unusual circumstances and/or expenses include: extraordinary medical expenses; expenses to care for the elderly, the handicapped, or people with special needs; child-care expenses (some institutions consider private education expenses, especially for areas of low-performing public schools); bankruptcies and back taxes; large one-time payments; lay-offs, retirements, and resignations; and cost-of-attendance adjustments for travel, books and supplies, or living expenses. If you have lost your job since you completed the needs analysis document and wish to inquire about additional aid, inform the college or university that your child is planning to attend about your economic situation. You can expect that the institution will require documentation verifying your current income. Most institutions have standard policies in place that allow for the use of projected income.

RESPONDING TO THE AWARD LETTER

Accept, decline, appeal, or seek clarification. These are the possible responses to an Award Letter. Accepting an award is usually as simple as signing and returning the Award Letter, although, as we mentioned earlier, additional application forms for specific funds or promissory notes for loans may be required. Declining an award is almost as important as accepting an award. Because funds are limited, schools attempt to redirect declined awards to other needy and eligible students. Most awards must be declined in writing. Usually, this is as simple as marking a box on the Award Letter that states the aid is being declined, signing the letter, and returning it to the school. Keep in mind that some schools may redirect funds if you do not respond by a certain date.

You may also reject or decline certain types of aid offered. For instance, you may wish to accept a Federal Work-Study award but decline a loan, or you may wish to accept only a portion of a specific award. For example, your child may have been offered a Federal Stafford Loan of $3,500. If, after carefully reviewing your budget and resources, you determine that it's possible to get by on less, you may choose to borrow only $2,000 per semester. Always carefully consider declining a grant, since a grant is money that does not have to be paid back or earned. No matter what the situation, you should respond to all aid offers made and, if possible, provide a short reason why any aid is being rejected.

When your child receives the Award Letter, you may feel that the offer is insufficient or you may wish to request a change in the types of aid that have been awarded (for example, replace a loan with work). You may want to discuss the treatment of a private scholarship or apprise the aid administrator of special family circumstances that may affect the award. Any of these situations necessitates a discussion with the financial aid administrator. If you are unhappy, unsatisfied, or simply confused about your child's aid offer, contact the school. Furthermore, if you have a delicate or complicated situation, schedule an appointment to meet with an aid administrator and, if necessary, bring any relevant information or documentation to the appointment.

Never reject a preferred school or, worse yet, decide not to proceed with your child's education, on the basis of insufficient financial aid. Instead, consult with an aid administrator and discuss possible alternatives. Aid administrators work diligently to ensure that deserving students are not denied access to higher education for financial reasons. They try to be sensitive to special circumstances, but to do that, they must be aware special circumstances exist.

Appealing

If you feel that an aid award is not sufficient, you should contact the aid office immediately to discuss your concerns and ask for "reconsideration." Start with the aid office at the school your child most wants to attend—if you can work things out with them, you will be set. If not, go to the second choice and so on. Do not try to get into a bidding war—these are rarely productive.

Always try first to contact the Financial Aid Office directly, not the Admission Office, not an alumnus, and not the president of the school! If you have trouble getting through, keep trying—it's a busy time. But if you can't get in touch within a week, talk to the Admission Office and see if they can help facilitate contact.

It is actually recommended that you visit the aid office of your number one college in person. Be courteous rather than demanding. The most effective attitude is to tell the aid counselor that you personally came to see him with the intention of trying to "make things work" financially, so your child can attend that college. Have copies of all your documents and any information that supports your appeal on hand when you do talk with the aid officer. If you have updated information, such as a more recent tax return, have that available as well.

> If you plan to appeal your aid award, avoid using the term "negotiate." Aid administrators don't like to be compared to used car salesmen.

Why else should you file an appeal? Some private colleges have an appeal policy that they will meet or match any award offer from a similar college. Will your college do the same? There is no harm in asking the question. If your Federal Supplemental Educational Opportunity Grant is lower than $2,000 (average award), ask if it can be increased (the maximum award is $4,000.) Also, many institutions have set aside institutional need-based grant funds that are not advertised. Go ahead and ask (appeal) for some of those dollars, especially if a school has left you with unmet need. Be prepared to also talk about financing options, but only after you have determined that there is no more grant aid available.

Don't expect an answer on the spot, but do ask when you might expect a decision and how that decision will be communicated. Assuming you contact the office in a timely manner, you should expect an answer to an aid appeal prior to the school's reply date. If you don't get one by then, ask for an extension to the reply date.

FINANCIAL AID BEYOND THE FIRST YEAR

Never assume that your child will receive similar financial aid awards in subsequent years, even if he or she plans to attend the same school. Awarding policies vary from school to school, and some schools award different types of aid packages depending upon grade level. Some schools award more grant aid and less self-help aid in the first year. As the student gains experience and the risk of failure diminishes, these types of schools increase the amount of loan or work offered in later years. Schools with discretionary institutional funds may reward high achievers with larger grant or merit-aid awards in future years. Other schools attempt to maintain the level of assistance offered to incoming first-year students throughout their school career. Don't be afraid to ask the financial aid administrator about the school's awarding policies.

HOW AND WHEN FINANCIAL AID IS PAID

Part of the award notification process includes an explanation of how and when the financial aid is paid. Financial aid can be paid using a number of different methods. Typically, a school credits financial aid funds to your child's school account to pay for school charges, such as tuition and fees. If you have remaining financial aid funds owed to you, the school pays you the balance, usually by issuing you a check. This money can be used to pay for education expenses like books and supplies, transportation costs, off-campus room and board, and miscellaneous personal items.

Generally, the Award Letter reflects the amount of aid that can be received for the entire academic year. The aid offered, though, must be disbursed in increments rather than in one lump sum. If your child's school is on a quarter system, one third of your financial assistance is usually disbursed at the beginning of the fall quarter, another third at the beginning of the winter quarter, and the remaining third at the beginning of the spring quarter. If he or she is attending a school on a semester system, one half of the aid is usually disbursed at the beginning of the fall semester, and the rest at the beginning of the spring semester.

WHAT'S NEXT?

Once you have accepted the school's offer of financial assistance, you also need to be aware of some issues related to the receipt of such aid.

➢ **The amount of grant aid your child receives in excess of the cost of tuition, fees, and course-related expenses, such as books and supplies, is generally considered to be taxable income and, as such, must be reported on his or her U.S. income tax return.**

➢ **A work-study award simply means that your child is eligible to earn that amount of money during the award year.** Before he or she can be paid, the student must obtain a work-study position and then work the hours necessary to earn the full amount of the award. work-study does not mean your child will get paid for studying.

➢ **You may be required to submit a separate loan application to apply for and receive money from the Federal Stafford Loan Program or PLUS Loan Program.** The school's financial aid office can provide you with the application materials and information about participating lenders. Many of these loan applications are now available on the Web, allowing for quicker processing.

CHAPTER.

9

If I Only Knew...

FAST FACTS

➤ **Don't let your son or daughter wait until his or her senior year to look for schools.** Waiting until this point will limit your options. Instead, start researching schools during your child's junior year.

➤ **Don't wait until your son or daughter is accepted to a school before making a visit.** Prior to applying, be sure to visit each school that is on the "under serious consideration" list.

➤ **Search for private schools that offer tuition reductions.** Strong SAT scores can result in your child receiving a scholarship that would make tuition at a private institution more affordable than a state-funded institution.

➤ **Find the schools not everyone is applying to.** There are hundreds of small colleges and universities out there that families pass over because they aren't the most popular or don't carry the prestige that others might. What many people fail to realize is that these schools are more likely to make some concessions so the cost of an education is affordable to low- and middle-income families.

Applying for financial aid can be very daunting, especially if you don't have someone to turn to who has been through it. To help alleviate your apprehensions, Peterson's interviewed five families who went through the financial aid process. Not only do these families share their experiences— both good and bad—but they also reveal what they would do differently if they could do it again. If you can learn from their experiences, you will be better able to use the financial aid system to your advantage. Note that we have changed the names of the families to protect their privacy.

THE CRISWELL FAMILY

Karole Criswell can finally see the light at the end of the tunnel. Of her three children, two have graduated from college, and the third is entering her sophomore year. But what makes this widowed mother's story so amazing is that even though she lives on a fixed income, she sent all three girls to school without the benefit of any financial aid. How? By sending all three to state universities.

Criswell admits that she didn't spend much time looking into financial aid. "I just assumed that if I owned a home and had money in the bank," she says, "I wouldn't be eligible." Her daughters' high school counselors did not offer much guidance regarding financial aid, either. Rather, they helped the girls narrow down their college choices based on what Criswell could afford to spend out-of-pocket.

Of the schools the guidance counselors suggested, Criswell felt the Cost of Attendance was most reasonable at public schools. So, instead of letting her children take out student loans, she encouraged them to focus on public schools in their home state of Pennsylvania. Ultimately, the older daughters enrolled at Penn State and the youngest, Robin, headed for West Chester University.

However, Robin's first choice was a school in Connecticut. Although it sent her an acceptance letter, the cost of tuition, room and board, and fees at the private, out-of-state college proved to be more than Criswell could afford. Knowing how much her daughter wanted to enroll at the Connecticut school, she contacted the school's financial aid office by phone and explained her situation. Criswell also asked her accountant to send the school a follow-up letter. This, however, was probably a mistake and may have given the staff the impression that Criswell didn't need financial aid as much as she claimed if she could afford an accountant. Ultimately, Robin decided to attend West Chester so she and her mother could avoid taking out loans. "We all have disappointments in life," says Criswell, "but we get over them."

Looking back on her experiences, Criswell regrets that she didn't understand the financial aid process, which meant that her daughters were limited in their choice of colleges. If she had it all to do again, she would do three things differently.

> ➤ She wouldn't have allowed her kids to wait until senior year to look for schools because this limited the number of colleges they were able to consider. Instead, she would have started them early in their junior year, so they would have the time to explore a wider range of schools.

> ➤ Criswell would have taken each of her children to see potential colleges before they sent in their applications—all three girls waited until after they had been accepted to make their college visits.

> ➤ Criswell realizes now just how little she knew about the financial aid process. "I should have gone to the colleges and spoken to someone about our options," she says.

If I Only Knew This About College Textbooks . . .

➢ Buy books early, buy from other students directly, and check local bookstores. Many books can be borrowed from local libraries and kept for entire semesters.

➢ Purchase used textbooks. Purchasing used textbooks is much less expensive than purchasing new books.

➢ Will the bookstore buy books back at the end of the semester? How are returned books valued? Is the condition of the book considered? Asking these questions could help you maximize the monies for which you are eligible.

THE GOING FAMILY

Most students rely on their parents to figure out how to get financial aid. But what happens when your parents are immigrants who don't speak much English? "I had to do everything on my own," says Dy Anne Going.

Going began thinking about financial aid in the middle of her junior year of high school. "My parents make a modest income, and there are two of us going to college at the same time (she has a twin brother), so I knew there was going to be financial aid." Going spent a lot of time in her guidance counselor's office, learning as much as she could about financial aid. Thanks to her counselor, she discovered her home state of New Jersey's Equal Opportunity Fund (EOF). The Fund provides grant money and academic assistance to disadvantaged residents of the state who can demonstrate both financial need and the motivation to pursue higher education.

Going also contacted the financial aid offices of the schools she applied to whenever she had questions. She was surprised by the aid awards she received from New Jersey's Montclair State and Rutgers Universities. "I didn't think I was going to get all that help money-wise," she says. She chose Rutgers, and in her second year she was again surprised by how large her package was. Besides the EOF grant, a Perkins Loan, and a subsidized loan, Going's aid package included work-study. "I've gotten $2,000 a year in work-study. That's been helpful." While she has used some of her work-study money to pay bills, Going is saving the majority of it to pay off her loans after graduation.

Going has gone through the application process twice now. "So far, it's gone pretty smoothly," she reflects. And while she wasn't afraid to ask questions of financial aid officers and her high school guidance counselor, she believes the process would have been easier if her parents spoke better English. "They would have supported me more, given me more advice," says Going.

She offers two pieces of advice to families who are applying for financial aid:

> ➤ "The sooner you can start the process, the better. If you wait until you're a senior, you're just going to panic."

> ➤ "Keep all of your paperwork from each school in a separate file when you're sending out financial aid applications. As the days went by, I could check to see if I was on the right track."

THE WILK FAMILY

Bernadette Wilk's daughter, Tiffany, had high SAT scores, strong grades, and plenty of extracurricular activities. "Everything," says Wilk, "that you were supposed to do to get all the money you could get. We expected the world to open up and give her everything."

At first, the Wilks were thrilled when Tiffany received merit awards from Lehigh and Lafayette Universities. But the awards—$3,000 per year—were not enough to make a significant difference. Tuition, room and board, fees, and transportation costs were going to total nearly $30,000 a year. Wilk says that when you're looking at such a large expense, "It's not about what the college is giving you, it's about what you have left to pay."

The Wilks took the next natural step: they applied for need-based aid. Wilk and her husband were proud that they had paid off the mortgage on their home a few years earlier. But every financial aid officer the Wilks spoke to had the same response: "For the equity that you have in the house, you can send three children to this school." Need-based aid would not be available to them. In the end, the Wilks took out a home equity loan in order to send their daughter to college. Rather than be bitter about it, though, Wilk says, "You owe your child an education, so you need to put in some of your own money to show your child the value of it."

To offset costs, Wilk had several recommendations:

➤ "Look into private scholarships. There are a lot of scholarships out there—religious, cultural, heritage affiliations—but you have to search them out."

➤ "Look into private schools that offer tuition reductions. Because of Tiffany's strong SAT score, Rider University offered to knock enough off the top to make tuition and room and board equal to that of a state university. But parents beware, if your child does not maintain an academic average, you lose it all!"

➤ "Don't rush to pay off your house. It isn't worth it."

THE HROUDA FAMILY

Marie Hrouda's son, Matt, received aid packages from ten different colleges. So when the Hrouda sat down to compare the awards, they quickly realized that they had to get organized. "You can't just look at the numbers and go from paper to paper," she says. "You have to actually put it up on a computer screen and look at the college, the tuition, the room and board."

The Hroudas, who live in New Jersey, initially were impressed by the large package offered by a well-known private university in Massachusetts. "But people fail to take into consideration all the extra expenses that go along with college," says Hrouda. "Everyone seems to think that the amount of money in the college guide is what it's going to cost. They don't add up all the other little incidentals that come along." These oft-forgotten costs include traveling home for the holidays and visits, parents' weekend, and medical expenses. "When you factor those things in," says Hrouda, "you have to look at a different picture than the school that is just 10 minutes away."

Hrouda went through the financial aid process with two other children a decade ago. But when it came time to apply for Matt, she discovered that things had changed dramatically. "More forms to fill out, they ask you more questions, they ask for what your children have in their savings accounts. They don't make the financial aid process 'people-friendly.'" Realizing how critical it is to understand the questions that are asked on the financial aid forms, the Hroudas hired a financial aid adviser.

When it came time to compare aid packages, the Hroudas created a spreadsheet on their home computer with three types of columns: expenses (tuition, room and board, and transportation); aid (subsidized and unsubsidized loans, work-study, and scholarships); and unmet need. "Nothing overwhelming," says Hrouda, who used her spreadsheet to help her son choose Villanova.

Marie Hrouda has the following advice for parents:

➤ "Organize yourself by making a binder for each school in which you're interested."

➤ "Visit each school's financial aid office."

➤ "Write down your impressions about each school after each visit—otherwise you will start mixing up who said what and how much he said."

If I Only Knew This About Credit Cards. . .

➢ If you have substantial credit card debt, remember that the needs analysis process does not give consideration to credit card debt in the typical calculations. Your best course of action is to complete the FAFSA and then establish a relationship with the university's financial aid office and explain your situation. Different institutions have different policies on how they will respond to these situations.

➢ If paying tuition by credit card, be aware of any additional costs charged by the university or a third-party servicer to cover the costs they incur for accepting credit cards. The fee may range from 1 to 3 percent of the amount charged and is in addition to the interest charge on your credit card bill.

➢ If paying tuition with a credit card in order to receive "frequent flyer miles," compare the interest you will pay for charging the tuition versus the value of the free miles. If you decide to charge $5,000 of tuition and pay it off in one year at an interest rate of 1.25 percent per month, you will spend approximately $406 in interest. Are the "frequent flyer miles" worth $406?

THE REYNOLDS FAMILY

When it comes to finding financial aid, you might think that Bob Reynolds has an advantage over most families because he's an accountant. It turns out, though, that the opposite is true. "I didn't know what to expect," he says of applying for aid for his stepdaughter. But it didn't take long before he learned "to forget the government unless you're at the poverty level, except for loans." Reynolds's experience has shown him that middle-class families who own a home and make a living that allows them to raise a family comfortably won't get much federal assistance.

Reynolds's stepdaughter was open to both public and private schools, and no specific school stood out as a "first choice." Instead, the final decision of where she would go to college would depend on the financial aid packages she received. As an accountant, Reynolds has seen his share of families who take out large loans to put their kids through college. "But I didn't want her or me saddled with a lot of debt," he recalls. So Reynolds went to work securing private scholarship money for his stepdaughter. Of the fifteen private and state scholarship programs his stepdaughter applied to, she only won one, what Reynolds calls an obscure, random state scholarship. "There's probably a lot more out there than people realize," he says, but he regrets that he had a difficult time locating legitimate scholarship programs.

The Reynoldses had to rely primarily on institutional financial aid and knew that they would have a better chance at winning scholarship money from colleges that most people have never heard of. So they applied to four small schools in Massachusetts, including Regis College. Once acceptance letters arrived, Reynolds got in touch with the financial aid offices by phone to negotiate aid packages. "If the college wants you," advises Reynolds, "they'll find something for you."

He found the staff at Regis to be "very pleasant" in the three or four calls he placed. And because it was a small school, each time he dealt with the same two people, one of whom was the school's financial aid director. Ultimately, he and Regis negotiated "a very nice package," says Reynolds. Regis offered his stepdaughter two grants based on academic performance, an off-campus work-study placement, and a subsidized Stafford Loan. "The first year," Reynolds recalls, "50 percent was covered, tuition and board." The remaining costs were made more manageable with a monthly payment plan.

Reynolds is about to start the process again with his son, a high school junior. What will he do differently this time? "I'm starting earlier, looking at potential colleges that meet his needs." Also, Reynolds will encourage his son to apply to more schools and to visit more colleges for face-to-face interviews in the hopes of securing better financial aid packages.

His advice to other families is simple: Find those schools that not everyone is applying to. There are hundreds of small colleges out there that families pass over because they aren't the most popular or prestigious. What people don't realize is that these schools are the ones that are willing to make some concessions, so the cost of higher education is affordable to middle-class families.

Did You Know?

➤ Usually, institutional departmental scholarships are not transferable from department to department. If your child plans to change majors, talk to the institution's financial aid office to determine whether the change will impact his or her scholarship.

➤ Read and understand any campus housing contract. Are there penalties if students change their mind concerning where they want to live? Do they have to maintain a certain credit load to be eligible for campus housing? Are they allowed to change rooms without financial penalty?

➤ Be aware of financial aid penalties for withdrawing from classes. These are in addition to tuition penalties. If a student who received Title IV (federal) financial aid withdraws from all classes before the 60 percent point in the semester at most schools, the student may be required to repay some or all Title IV financial aid. This is dictated by a federal formula. Check with a financial aid counselor and ask specifically about how withdrawing from classes will affect your child's aid.

Now You Do!

A

Financial Aid Countdown Calendar

JUNIOR YEAR

Fall

➤ Now is the time to get serious about the colleges in which your child is interested. Meet with the guidance counselor to narrow down the choices. College visits are always a great idea as this will be the place your child will call home for the next four years!

➤ Make sure your child registers for the Preliminary SAT (PSAT).

➤ Check out local financial aid information nights in the area. Be sure to attend these valuable sessions, especially if this is the first time your family is sending someone off to college. Try to become familiar with common financial aid terms. Start reviewing the literature available and begin to familiarize yourself with the various programs. A good booklet is published by the U.S. Department of Education, *The Student Guide*, and is available at any financial aid office or on the Web at http://studentaid.ed.gov/students/publications/student_guide/index.html.

➤ In October, make sure your child takes the PSAT/National Merit Scholarship Qualifying Test.

➤ Do some Web browsing and check out the many free scholarship search engines available. Also, head to the bookstore or library and pick up a copy of *Peterson's Scholarships, Grants & Prizes*. It features details on billions of dollars of aid from private sources.

➤ Contact the employers, unions, and church and fraternal organizations with which you have a connection to learn about possible scholarship opportunities.

➤ Check with the high school guidance counselor for the qualifications and deadlines of local scholarship awards. Many guidance counselors report that there are few applicants for these awards.

Winter

➤ Keep checking for scholarships! Remember that this is the one area over which you have control.

➤ Make sure your child registers and studies for the SAT and SAT Subject Tests.

Spring

➤ It's a great time to visit colleges, especially when their classes are in session. Remember that top ten list? Time to start narrowing it down.

➤ Review the requirements for local scholarships. What can your child do now and over the summer to improve his or her chances?

➤ Wish your child luck in taking the SATs!

➤ Help your child look for a summer job, especially one that ties in with college plans. For example, if he or she wants to major in premed, why not try for a job at a hospital or with a laboratory?

Summer

➤ College visit time! Ask your child: Is this where you see yourself getting your undergraduate degree? Can you adjust to the seasons, the town surrounding the campus, the distance from home, the college size? Does this school feel right for you and your child?

➤ Get a jump on college (and maybe save some money!) and enroll your child in a college course at the local community college. Or, better yet, have him or her do some extra prep work for the upcoming SAT!

SENIOR YEAR

Fall

➤ Once you have your child's top choices, make a list of what each college requires for admission and financial aid. Be sure your list includes all deadlines.

➤ Attend a financial aid information night presentation. Some of these sessions offer help in completing forms; others offer a broader view of the process. Contact the presenter (usually a local college financial aid professional) to be sure you are getting the information you need.

➤ Do any of these colleges require the PROFILE® financial aid application? Many private colleges use this form for institutional aid. You need to file this comprehensive form in late September or early October. Web site registration is free; however, PROFILE is a fee-based application.

➤ Don't falter now in your scholarship search. Make sure your child has the applications filed by the published deadlines.

➤ Register now if your child plans to retake the SAT.

➤ Most important, make sure your child starts to complete the college applications—the earlier, the better! Remember, accuracy and completeness are a must!

Winter

➤ Ensure all college applications are completed.

➤ Get the Free Application for Federal Student Aid (FAFSA). This is the key form for financial aid for every school across the country. Remember, watch the deadlines, but do not file until after January 1. Be sure to keep a copy of the form, whether you file electronically or with the paper application. Do you have questions? Call the local financial aid office. Also, many states have special toll-free call-in programs in January and February, Financial Aid Awareness Month.

➤ Be sure that each school's required forms are completed.

➤ As the letters of admission start to arrive, the Financial Aid Award Letters should be right behind them. Important question for parents: What is the bottom line? Remember, aid at a lower-cost state school will be less than a higher-cost private college. But what will you be required to pay? This can be confusing, so consider gift aid (scholarships and grants), student loans, and parent loans. The school with the lowest sticker price (tuition, fees, and room and board) might not be the best bargain when you look at the overall financial aid package.

Spring

➤ The financial aid package at your child's top choice just not enough? Call the Financial Aid Office and the Admissions Office. Talk it over. While schools don't like to bargain, they are usually willing to take a second look. Is there something unusual about your family's financial situation that might impact your ability to pay?

➤ By May 1, you must make your final decision. Notify the chosen college and find out what needs to happen next. Tell the other colleges you are not accepting their offers of admission and financial aid.

Summer

➤ Time to crunch the numbers. Get information from the college on the total charges for the coming fall term. Deduct the aid package and then plan for how the balance will be paid. Contact the college Financial Aid Office for the best parental loan program. If you want to arrange for a payment plan, contact the Business Office for further information. Most schools have deferred payment plans available for a nominal fee.

Congratulations! You made it! But, don't forget, you need to reapply for aid every year!

B

Top 19 Questions Parents and Students Should Ask

How many times after leaving the doctor's office have you said, "I forgot to ask about . . ."? Similarly, many families only remember the right questions to ask about college financial aid after they've completed a campus visit. The answers you receive from financial aid officers should enable you to decide which college is the best fit from a financial aid perspective. Also, pay close attention to how aid officers respond to follow-up questions. Look for informative, solution-oriented responses. For example, do college officials give enough detail to satisfy your needs, and do they take the time to problem-solve the question? Financial aid issues are often complex, so use the answers as your barometer for deciding if the school is financial aid "family friendly."

> Ask your questions directly and consistently. Do not get caught up in the financial aid jargon.

We want you to be a "thinking parent," so jot down any related questions that pop into your head while you read these recommended questions. You should approach applying for financial aid with the same kind of attention as you do when applying for admission.

We've repeated these questions for you on page 173. When you visit colleges, tear out the questions from the book and refer to them when you meet with a financial aid counselor.

School Flexibility

Q. What is your policy regarding "projected year income"?

A. Projected year income is a term used by aid offices when you request a reexamination of your financial condition based on a loss of income. For example, at the time of completing the financial aid application both parents were employed. However, since then one parent has lost his or her job or has had a serious reduction of income (i.e., stock market losses or long-term disability). Ask the Financial Aid Office if it will consider revising the original financial aid analysis and bottom-line Expected Family Contribution and use "projected year" earnings rather than prior year earnings, which the family can no longer expect to receive. Not all schools will accept this appeal request, but federal regulations do allow for this type of consideration on a case-by-case basis. If the school does consider this kind of appeal, be prepared to prove (document) your loss of income/revenue and provide reasonable estimates of future earnings.

Policies

Q. What is the minimum course load required to maintain grants?

A. Most colleges require undergraduate students to carry a full-time course load of at least 12 credits a term in order to receive a "full" financial aid award. However, many students reduce their course load in order to protect their grade point average, hoping that taking fewer credits will lead to higher grades. Other students will drop a course with which they are having difficulty, not realizing it could jeopardize their financial aid eligibility. You must know the school's policies and ask what the requirements are before classes begin. Penalties also can be applied to students who only receive merit funds. In fact, many schools have tougher policies governing academic merit awards than for other forms of grants. In some instances, institutional scholarships may be reduced or canceled if the student drops any courses. Use caution. Any reduction of course work should first be discussed with a financial aid counselor.

Q. **May I meet with a financial aid counselor today?**

A. While on your college visits, you will probably attend orientation sessions given by admissions staff representatives. You may also speak to a professor or an athletic coach. But have you made an appointment to see a financial aid counselor? Most parents haven't. The thinking parent will. You need to introduce yourself to a financial aid counselor early in the admissions and financial aid cycle so that the Financial Aid Office can become familiar with you and your needs. While speaking to the counselor, confirm the priority filing dates for all required financial aid applications.

If you have a story to tell, this first meeting is the time to tell it. Try to develop a one-to-one relationship with your financial aid counselor. This is your opportunity to gauge what kind of a person your financial aid counselor is. How experienced is she? Will she be assigned to work with you for the year? Does she listen and understand your concerns and issues? Can she explain how to file for additional assistance? What does the institution look for in making award adjustments? Is the counselor aware of any discretionary institutional funds in the event you require additional funding?

While in the aid office, ask the counselor to review your file with you and explain how your Expected Family Contribution was determined. Errors can be made, so you must make certain that correct information is being used in the needs-analysis process. If anything has changed financially or medically since you filed your application, let the counselor know, and if possible, have any supporting records available. Aid adjustments can be made during this meeting. The key point is to establish a relationship with a financial aid counselor as soon as possible. Your first campus visit is an ideal opportunity.

Family Matters

Q. Do you consider stepparents' income when analyzing an application for aid?

A. Many students come from divorced families. Financial aid issues for divorced families can be very complex. Federal needs analysis methodology requires stepparent information to be included when completing the FAFSA. There really is no choice here, and if you do not report stepparent income, your application will be delayed for processing. It is better to appeal later than stop the initial aid review. A financial aid counselor may be able to "override" stepparent income if you appeal (a valid reason might be the short duration of the marriage). It's not guaranteed, but sometimes it is possible.

Q. Do you consider an ex-spouse's income for institutional financial aid consideration?

A. This is an important question to ask. Many private colleges will require this information. If the college requires a CSS/PROFILE® application in addition to the FAFSA, you will be required to report far more family financial information than on the FAFSA. It may not seem fair, but colleges that award significant institutional funds need as much financial information as possible to ensure the neediest students receive priority consideration.

Getting Money

Q. We have not filed our income taxes yet, and your financial aid deadline date is fast approaching. What should we do?

A. File your FAFSA right now, using estimated figures and make corrections later (or the school may), if necessary, once your tax forms are filed. Ask the college what policy they have for this situation in case it arises.

Q. Do you leave unmet need in your financial aid package?

A. According to the Advisory Committee on Student Financial Assistance, families of low-income, college-qualified high school graduates face annual unmet need of $3,800 for public college expenses not covered by student aid, including work-study and student loans.

Most schools will try to convince you that they meet the full cost of attendance when awarding student aid. Most don't actually do it. So ask what is the composition of the financial aid package? How is the school defining a "full" award? You need to know the percentage of grant and self-help assistance (loan or job).

If the school does not meet full need, sometimes called "gapping," ask if you will be expected to take out more than one loan each year. If you are offered more than one loan, proceed cautiously. Is this the school's best offer, or can they do better? This should be the time to sit down with the financial aid counselor and find a way not to borrow from more than one loan source, if possible.

Q. What is the average debt burden of those students who graduate, and what is the average time it takes to graduate?

A. Other factors to consider when comparing college aid offers are total expected debt burden based on Expected Family Contribution and length of time to graduate, which could extend loan borrowing. The average loan debt of a public university undergraduate is $16,000 to $17,000 upon graduation, and the majority of students take five years to graduate. The average loan debt of a private college can be $24,000 or more. You need to find out if the school makes every effort to minimize student and parent borrowing. Most schools increase the loan portion of a student's aid package every year as eligibility for loan programs increase. If this is the case, will the school also reduce their grant award each year?

Q. Does your grant aid to freshmen remain constant for their remaining three or four years?

A. Sometimes, the best financial aid deal is from the college that is the most consistent with its award over all four years of a student's enrollment. Don't be surprised to find your freshman-year grant is gradually reduced each subsequent year, especially if you expect your income to remain relatively the same or to increase. You can be certain that most schools' costs will go up every year. Ask the schools to clearly explain their policy of upper-class grant awarding.

What if your child takes five years to graduate? Will institutional grants be eliminated in their fifth year, even if they maintain an exceptional grade point average? This situation occurs more often than you might expect. See if the school will show you typical Award Letters for students who received aid over a four-year period as well as for students who received aid over a five-year period.

Keeping Costs Down

Q. Do you offer a tuition discount for families with more than one child attending your school at the same time?

A. Research shows that many institutions offer tuition discounts if more than one sibling is enrolled at the same institution at the same time. A 25 percent discount is the rule of thumb. So ask if you are eligible for reduced tuition if multiple children attend the school.

Q. On average, how much have your tuition and room and board costs increased over the past four years?

A. Research shows that families place a great deal of importance on higher education, but they are unsure how much college really costs. Likewise, many families do not know how much costs increase every year. In recent years, families have seen tuition increase by more than 10 percent each year. Although tuition increases have leveled off, it is still common to see yearly increases of 2 to 5 percent. Add in room and board expenses, which increase between 5 and 8 percent each year, and we are talking about big bucks.

Q. Do you provide aid for summer school?

A. Ask if the school will offer any assistance with summer costs. If your child can find a way to take 3 to 6 credits per summer, you can reduce college costs by as much as 25 percent. Although most colleges will award summer loans, it may be possible to receive some small grant assistance for the summer. You also might be able to save money on books because used books are more available at that time of year. You will also save on room and board expenses if your child lives at home. A local college near your home may have just the courses needed during the summer session.

Scholarship Awareness

Q. Will an outside scholarship reduce my aid award, especially institutional grants or scholarships?

A. Every school is different in how it treats a financial aid award when an outside scholarship is received. For example, if the financial aid award from the school is $10,000, and of that, $6,000 is grant money and the rest is self-help, what happens to the overall award if your child receives an outside scholarship? Will the college replace its grants with the outside award? Will the outside scholarship be used to fill in any "gap" in need? If not, will loans be reduced first? Can the school reduce your Expected Family Contribution to absorb the outside scholarship? Many parents don't have the Expected Family Contribution that the Central Processing System calculates is available. This is where an appeal should be considered, so that outside scholarship funds are not in jeopardy.

Q. Is my institutional scholarship renewable?

A. If your child is fortunate enough to receive an institutional scholarship, you will need to read the fine print regarding what needs to be done to retain the scholarship. Make sure you know the duration of the scholarship and required minimum grade point average. Is the scholarship good for just one year? Will it increase if tuition increases, or is it for a fixed dollar amount? If the scholarship is not renewable, ask how the school will assist you with making up the difference in the following year. Will your child be considered for alternative scholarships as an upper-class student?

Q. Can lost scholarship eligibility be reinstated?

A. Sometimes, students can lose a scholarship after attending college for just one term, especially if they fail to maintain a minimum grade point average. Quite often, there are different minimum grade requirements for receiving federal, state, and institutional assistance. If the student gets back on track during the next term, will the scholarship be reinstated? You need to know what each fund source requires. Failure to do so can cost parents and students thousands of dollars. It is critical to be informed of each college's scholarship requirements. Determine what appeal process exists if your child has a problem with scholarship maintenance.

Q. Do you award departmental scholarships for upper-class students?

A. The majority of scholarship applicants are denied merit-based assistance. Don't give up hope. Some institutions award upper-class scholarships that your child can apply for following his or her freshman year. In addition, specific departments within the institution award scholarships based on a student's major. Check with the financial aid office for more information.

Out-of-State Schools

Q. How long will it take to become a state resident? Do you have tuition reciprocity agreements?

A. Do you really want to save a lot of tuition money? During your campus visit, see what it will take to establish in-state residency status. Learn what the requirements are to only pay in-state tuition. Normally, the registrar's office or the cashier's office will have the best information on this issue. There have been many students who have gained in-state status while attending the institution first as an out-of-state student. Usually, there are residency committees that will hear a family's appeal. Don't be too timid to ask what you need to do. Make sure to read the school's catalog on this policy question.

Reciprocity agreements are tuition discount agreements between states, institutions, and even regions. For example, the state of Maryland has no degree program in textile fiber engineering. However, Georgia Institute of Technology does, and a resident of Maryland majoring in this field can attend Georgia Tech as an in-state resident. By not having to pay out-of-state tuition, the student will save more than $30,000 in four years. Another example is the Western Interstate Commission for Higher Education, which has agreements to allow a student to pay in-state tuition at an out-of-state school if his or her field of study is not offered in the student's home state. Presently, fifteen states participate in this program (Alaska, Arizona, California, Colorado, Hawaii, Idaho, Montana, Nevada, New Mexico, North Dakota, Oregon, South Dakota, Utah, Washington, and Wyoming).

Finding Campus Employment

Q. How many job opportunities are there on campus?

A. Ask what percentage of on-campus jobs is based on need versus those based on non-need. In other words, if you applied for financial aid and were denied, are there still jobs available for students from families like yours? What types of jobs are there?

Are there any that are more academically oriented than others? What is the typical pay and how many hours is a student expected to work? It's important to ask if there is a campus employment office that assists students with finding jobs. Ask if job listings can be e-mailed to you in late summer, so your child can apply and interview before the fall rush. See if the college has job listings available on its Web site. Also keep in mind that college students typically have less free time to work each week than high school students. Can your child reasonably be expected to earn as much as the school has offered you?

Q. **Will on- or off-campus job earnings affect grant eligibility?**

A. If you are offered a need-based federal work-study job, consider this job over a non-federal work-study job that you may be considering. Federal work-study jobs are not counted as a financial resource when you reapply for financial aid. Non-federal jobs are counted and may reduce your aid award the following year. In general, a student can earn about $3,000 per year before it has an impact on financial aid eligibility. Another advantage of federal work-study is resume-building while in school. Your child also may be able to work off campus in a job that is supported by work-study funds.

TOP 19 QUESTIONS PARENTS AND STUDENTS SHOULD ASK

1. What is your policy regarding "projected year income"?

2. What is the minimum course load required to maintain grants?

3. May I meet with a financial aid counselor today?

4. Do you consider stepparents' income when analyzing an application for aid?

5. Do you consider an ex-spouse's income for institutional financial aid consideration?

6. We have not filed our income taxes yet, and your financial aid deadline date is fast approaching. What should we do?

7. Do you leave unmet need in your financial aid package?

8. What is the average debt burden of those students who graduate, and what is the average time it takes to graduate?

9. Does your grant aid to freshmen remain constant for their remaining three years?

10. Do you offer a tuition discount for families with more than one child attending your school at the same time?

11. On average, how much have your tuition and room and board costs increased over the past four years?

12. Do you provide aid for summer school?

13. Will an outside scholarship reduce my aid award, especially institutional grants or scholarships?

14. Is my institutional scholarship renewable?

15. Can lost scholarship eligibility be reinstated?

16. Do you award departmental scholarships for upper-class students?

17. How long will it take to become a state resident? Do you have tuition reciprocity agreements?

18. How many job opportunities are there on campus?

19. Will on- or off-campus job earnings affect grant eligibility?

C

Glossary

A

Ability to Benefit: Postsecondary institutions may not award federal aid to students without a high school or equivalency diploma unless the student has demonstrated that he or she can benefit from the education offered.

Academic Competitiveness Grant (ACG): Federal grant program open to U.S. citizens who are Pell Grant recipients and enrolled as first- or second-year students in a qualifying program of study. The recipient must have completed a "rigorous" secondary school program (or alternative) as outlined by the U.S. Department of Education. Students must demonstrate financial need for the grant.

Academic Credit: The unit of measurement an institution gives to a student when he/she fulfills course or subject requirement(s) as determined by the institution.

Academic Year (AY): This is a measure of the academic work to be accomplished by a student. The school defines its own academic year, but the federal regulations set minimum standards to determine federal financial aid awards. For instance, the academic year must be at least 30 weeks of instructional time in which a full-time student is expected to complete at least 24 semester or trimester credit hours or 36 quarter credit hours or 900 clock hours.

Accrual Date: The date on which interest charges begin to be applied to the loan principal.

Accrued Interest: Interest which accumulates on the outstanding balance of a loan.

Adjusted Available Income: The portion of family income remaining after deducting federal, state, and local taxes, a living allowance, and other factors used in the Federal Need Analysis Methodology.

Adjusted Gross Income (AGI): All taxable income as reported on a U.S. income tax return.

Advanced Placement (AP) Program: A series of examinations demonstrating a student's proficiency in a subject area, for which some postsecondary institutions offer credit.

Alternative Loan: An educational loan that is made by a private lender to a student borrower and is not guaranteed by either the federal or state government.

AmeriCorps: *See National and Community Service.*

Amortization: The application of payments to both the loan interest and principal over time in periodic installments.

Appeal: The action taken by a family should it determine that the offered financial aid package is inadequate—especially in the case of a parent's or spouse's death, unemployment, or other factors that seriously alter a family's financial status. A financial aid officer will review the components of the family's EFC and determine whether or not the family's special circumstances warrant a revision to one or more of the EFC components.

Assets: Cash on hand in checking and savings accounts; trusts, stocks, bonds, and other securities; and real estate (excluding home), income-producing property, business equipment, and business inventory. Considered in determining EFC under the regular formula.

Associate Degree: A degree given for successful completion of courses of study at a two-year college.

Award Letter: A means of notifying financial aid applicants of the assistance being offered. The Award Letter usually provides information on the types and amounts of aid offered, as well as specific program information, student responsibilities, and the conditions that govern the award. Generally provides students with the opportunity to accept or decline the aid offered. *Also see Financial Aid Notification.*

Award Year: The period of time between July 1 of one year and June 30 of the following year.

B

Bachelor's Degree: The degree given for successful completion of the undergraduate curriculum at a four-year college or a university. Also called baccalaureate degree.

Base Year: For need analysis purposes, the base year is the 12-month calendar year preceding the award year (e.g., 2008 is the base year for the 2009–2010 award year).

BIA Grant: *See Bureau of Indian Affairs (BIA) Grant.*

Bureau of Indian Affairs (BIA) Grant: A federal grant program administered by the Bureau of Indian Affairs for needy students who are members of an Indian, Eskimo, or Aleut tribe and enrolled in accredited institutions in pursuit of an undergraduate or graduate degree.

Business Assets: Property that is used in the operation of a trade or business, including real estate, inventories, buildings, machinery and other equipment, patents, franchise rights, and copyrights. Considered in determining a family's EFC under the regular formula unless the business is family-owned and controlled with no more than 100 full-time employees or equivalent.

C

Campus-Based Programs: The term commonly applied to those U.S. Department of Education federal student aid programs administered directly by institutions of postsecondary education. Includes: Federal Supplemental Educational Opportunity Grant (FSEOG), Federal Work-Study (FWS), and Federal Perkins Loan Programs.

Cancellation (of loan): The condition that exists when a borrower of a federal student loan has fulfilled requirements to permit cancellation, or writing off, of a designated portion of the principal and interest.

Capitalization (of interest): When accrued and unpaid interest is added to the principal amount of the loan.

Certificate: The formal acknowledgment of successful completion of a particular program or course of study, particularly in a vocational school, trade school, or junior college.

Citizen: A person who owes allegiance to the United States. Most state and federal financial aid programs are considered domestic assistance programs and are available only to citizens, nationals, and permanent residents of the U.S., and people who are in this country for other than temporary purposes. Citizens of the Republic of the Marshall Islands, the Federated States of Micronesia, and the Republic of Palau are eligible for Federal Pell Grant, FSEOG, and FWS only.

CLEP: *See College-Level Examination Program.*

Clock Hour: The unit of measurement some institutions give for fulfilling course requirements.

COA: *See Cost of Attendance.*

College-Level Examination Program (CLEP): A series of examinations demonstrating a student's proficiency in a subject area, for which some postsecondary institutions offer credit.

Commercial Lender: A commercial bank, savings and loan association, credit union, stock savings bank, trust company, or mutual savings bank. Can act as a lender for the Federal Family Education Loan (FFEL) Program.

Commuter Student: A student who does not live on campus; typically, commuter refers to a student living at home with his or her parents, but can also mean any student who lives off campus.

Consolidation Loan: A loan made to enable a borrower with different types of education loans to obtain a single loan with one interest rate and one repayment schedule. Federal Perkins Loans, Federal Stafford Loans (Subsidized and Unsubsidized), Direct Loans, Health Education Assistance Loans (HEAL), Health Professions Student

Loans, and Loans for Disadvantaged Students may be combined for purposes of consolidation, subject to certain eligibility requirements. A consolidation loan pays off the existing loans; the borrower repays the consolidated loan.

Cost of Attendance (COA): In general, this includes the tuition and fees normally assessed a student, together with the institution's estimate of the cost of room and board, transportation and commuting costs, books and supplies, and miscellaneous personal expenses. In addition, student loan fees, dependent care, reasonable costs for a study-abroad or cooperative education program, and/or costs related to a disability may be included, when appropriate. Also referred to as cost of education or budget.

Credit (or Credit Hour): The unit of measurement some institutions give for fulfilling course requirements.

Custodial Parent: A single parent who has financially supported the student most in the previous twelve months. The custodial parent is the parent who will complete the financial aid applications and upon whose assets and income the EFC will be calculated.

D

DANTES: *See Defense Activity for Non-Traditional Education Support.*

Debt Burden: A student's repayment obligation or the amount of loans included in a student's financial aid package.

Default (Federal Perkins Loan): A loan for which the borrower failed to make an installment payment when due and such failure persisted (was not cured either by payment or other appropriate arrangements). The Department of Education considers a loan discharged in bankruptcy not to be in default.

Default (Federal Stafford, Direct, Federal PLUS, or Direct PLUS Loans): The failure of a borrower to make an installment payment when due, or to meet other terms of the promissory note under circumstances where the Department of Education or the pertinent guaranty agency finds it reasonable to conclude that the borrower no longer intends to honor the obligation to repay. The Department of Education considers a loan discharged in bankruptcy not to be in default.

Defense Activity for Non-Traditional Education Support (DANTES): A series of examinations sponsored by the military to help servicemen and women as well as non-military people obtain college credit for the knowledge and skills they have acquired.

Deferment (of loan): A condition during which payments of principal are not required, and, for Federal Perkins, Federal Subsidized Stafford, and Direct Subsidized Loans, interest does not accrue. The repayment period is extended by the length of the deferment period.

Departmental Scholarship: An award of gift assistance that is specifically designated for a recipient in a particular academic department within the institution.

Department of Education, U.S. (ED): The department of the federal government that administers assistance to students enrolled in postsecondary educational programs under the following programs: Federal Pell Grant, Academic Competitiveness Grants (ACG), National SMART Grants, Federal Perkins Loan, Federal Supplemental Educational Opportunity Grant (FSEOG), Federal Work-Study (FWS), Federal Family Education Loan (FFEL), and William D. Ford Federal Direct Loan.

Direct Loan (Subsidized and Unsubsidized): Long-term, low-interest loans administered by the Department of Education and institutions with a fixed interest rate. Direct Unsubsidized Loans can be used to replace EFC.

Disbursement: The process by which financial aid funds are made available to students for use in meeting educational and related living expenses.

E

Educational Benefits: Funds, primarily federal, awarded to certain categories of students (veterans, children of deceased veterans or other deceased wage earners, and students with physical disabilities) to help finance their postsecondary education regardless of their ability to demonstrate need in the traditional sense.

Education Expenses: *See Cost of Attendance.*

EFC: *See Expected Family Contribution.*

Eligibility Criteria: The specific conditions that a student must meet to qualify for financial assistance. In addition to demonstrating need for most programs, general eligibility criteria for federal student aid include, among other things, citizenship status and selective service registration. Individual programs may carry other specific eligibility requirements in addition to the general eligibility criteria.

Eligible Institution: An institution of higher education, vocational school, postsecondary vocational institution, or proprietary institution of higher education that meets all criteria for participation in the federal student aid programs.

Eligible Noncitizen: Person who, although not a U.S. citizen, qualifies for federal student aid in one of the following eligible categories: 1) U.S. permanent resident who has an Alien Registration Receipt Card (Form I-151 or I-551, usually referred to as green cards) or other evidence of admission for permanent residence; 2) Conditional permanent resident (I-151C); 3) Person designated as lawfully present in U.S. for other than a temporary purpose who has an Arrival-Departure Record (Form I-94) from the Bureau of Citizenship and Immigration Services stamped as refugee, granted asylum, indefinite parolee and/or humanitarian parolee, or Cuban-Haitian entrant; 5) Permanent resident of the Republic of Palau or citizen of the Republic of the Marshall Islands and the Federated States of Micronesia. Non-citizens who are not eligible for federal student aid include holders of Student Visas, Exchange Visitors Visas, G-Series Visas, or those who have only a Notice of Approval to Apply for Permanent Residence. *Also see Legal Resident and Residency Requirements.*

Eligible Program: A program of education or training that leads to a degree or a certificate at a school participating in one or more federal student aid programs. A student must be enrolled in an eligible program at an eligible school to receive federal student assistance.

Employment: With reference to financial aid, the opportunity for students to earn money to help pay for their education. Federal Work-Study is one program by which needy students can work to defray their educational expenses.

Endowment: Funds obtained and owned by the postsecondary institution that are invested so that the income from the investment can be used for various purposes, such as construction, research, and financial aid.

Enrolled: The completion of registration requirements (other than the payment of tuition and fees) at the institution the student is or will be attending; a correspondence school student must be accepted for admission and complete and submit one lesson to be considered enrolled.

Enrollment Status: At those institutions using semesters, trimesters, quarters, or other academic terms and measuring progress by credit hours, enrollment status equals a student's credit hour workload categorized as either full-time, three-quarter-time, half-time, or less-than-half-time.

Entitlement Program: Program that is funded sufficiently to ensure that all eligible applicants are guaranteed to receive maximum authorized awards. As long as the applicant meets all the eligibility requirements and is enrolled in an eligible program at an eligible institution, he or she will receive the award for which eligibility has been established.

Excelsior College Examinations: Formerly ACT/PEP, these exams are used to meet specific college degree requirements of Excelsior College and are accepted for college credit by approximately 1,000 colleges and universities. Excelsior College now administers these examinations worldwide.

Expected Family Contribution (EFC): The amount a student and his or her family are expected to pay toward the student's Cost of Attendance as calculated by a congressionally mandated formula known as Federal Methodology. The EFC is used to determine a student's eligibility for student financial assistance programs.

F

FAFSA: *See Free Application for Federal Student Aid.*

FAFSA Processor: An organization contracted by the Department of Education to provide the means for a student to apply for federal student aid. The FAFSA processor electronically enters the student's FAFSA data into a computer system and then transmits the data to the Central Processing System.

Federal Family Education Loan (FFEL) Program: The collective name for the Federal Stafford Loan (Subsidized and Unsubsidized), Federal PLUS Loan, and Federal Consolidation Loan Programs. Funds for these programs are provided by private lenders and the loans are guaranteed by the federal government.

Federal Methodology (FM): *See Federal Need Analysis Methodology.*

Federal Need Analysis Methodology: A standardized method for determining a student's ability to pay for postsecondary education expenses; also referred to as Federal Methodology (FM). The single formula for determining an Expected Family Contribution (EFC) for Pell Grants, Academic Competitiveness Grants, National SMART Grants, campus-based programs, FFEL Program, and Direct Loan Program; the formula is defined in statute.

Federal Pell Grant: A federal grant program for needy postsecondary students who have not yet received a baccalaureate or first-professional degree; administered by the U.S. Department of Education.

Federal Perkins Loan: One of the campus-based loan programs; a long-term, low interest loan program for both undergraduate and graduate students at a current interest rate of 5 percent.

Federal Stafford Loan (Subsidized and Unsubsidized): Long-term, low-interest loans administered by the Department of Education through private guaranty agencies. Fixed interest rate. Federal Unsubsidized Stafford Loans may be used to replace EFC.

Federal Supplemental Educational Opportunity Grant (FSEOG): One of the campus-based programs; grants to undergraduate students of exceptional financial need who have not completed their first baccalaureate degree and who are financially in need of this grant to enable them to pursue their education. Priority for FSEOG awards must be given to Federal Pell Grant recipients with the lowest EFCs.

Federal Work-Study Program (FWS): One of the campus-based programs; a part-time employment program that provides jobs for undergraduate and graduate students who are in need of such earnings to meet a portion of their educational expenses.

FFEL: *See Federal Family Education Loan Program.*

Financial Aid: General term that describes any source of student assistance other than the student or the student's family; funds awarded to a student to help meet postsecondary educational expenses. These funds are generally awarded on the basis of financial need and include scholarships, grants, loans, and employment.

Financial Aid Administrator: An individual who is responsible for preparing and communicating information pertaining to student loans, grants or scholarships, and employment programs, and for advising, awarding, reporting, counseling, and supervising office functions related to student financial aid. He or she is accountable to the various publics that are involved; is a manager or administrator who interprets and implements federal, state, and institutional policies and regulations; and is capable of analyzing student and employee needs and making changes where necessary.

Financial Aid Award Letter: An amount of financial or in-kind assistance offered to a student attending a postsecondary educational institution. This award may be in the form of one or more of the following types of financial aid: repayable loan, non-repayable grant and/or scholarship, and/or student employment.

Financial Aid Consultant: A person who, for a fee, provides a variety of services to students, including preparing the FAFSA and other financial aid forms, estimating the Expected Family Contribution (EFC), and estimating financial need.

Financial Aid Notification: The letter from the postsecondary institution that lets the student know whether or not aid has been awarded. If the student will be receiving assistance, the notification also describes the financial aid package. State agencies and private organizations may send students financial aid notifications separately from the postsecondary institution. *Also see Award Letter.*

Financial Aid Package: A financial aid award to a student comprised of a combination of forms of financial aid (loans, grants and/or scholarships, and/or employment).

Financial Need: The difference between the institution's Cost of Attendance and the family's ability to pay. Ability to pay is represented by the Expected Family Contribution for federal need-based aid and for many state and institutional programs.

Financial Need Equation: Cost of Attendance (COA) minus Expected Family Contribution (EFC) equals financial need (COA − EFC = Financial Need).

FM: *See Federal Need Analysis Methodology.*

Forbearance: Permitting the temporary cessation of repayments of loans, allowing an extension of time for making loan payments, or accepting smaller loan payments than were previously scheduled.

Foreign Student: A student from or owing allegiance to another country. Foreign students are not eligible for the basic federal programs, although there are categories of non-U.S. citizens who owe permanent allegiance to the United States and are eligible for student aid.

Formula: *See Need Analysis Formula.*

Free Application for Federal Student Aid (FAFSA): The financial aid application document completed by the student that collects household and financial information. The FAFSA is the foundation document for all federal need analysis computations and database matches performed for a student.

FSEOG: *See Federal Supplemental Educational Opportunity Grant.*

Full-Time Student: In general, one who is taking a minimum of 12 semester or quarter hours per academic term; 24 semester or 36 quarter hours per year at institutions using credits but not terms; or 24 clock hours per week at institutions that measure progress in clock hours.

FWS: *See Federal Work-Study Program.*

G

Gift Aid: Educational funds such as grants or scholarships that do not require repayment from present or future earnings. *Also see Grant.*

Grace Period: The period of time that begins when a loan recipient ceases to be enrolled at least half-time and ends when the repayment period starts. Loan principal need not be paid and interest does not accrue on subsidized loans during this period.

Grant: A type of financial aid that does not have to be repaid; usually awarded on the basis of need, possibly combined with some skills or characteristics the student possesses. *Also see Gift Aid.*

H

Health and Human Services, U.S. Department of (HHS): The section of the federal government that provides assistance to future health care practitioners. The Nursing Student Loan, Health Professions Student Loan, and Scholarships for Disadvantaged Students Program are among some of the aid programs administered by HHS.

Health Professions Programs: Federal student assistance programs administered by the U.S. Department of Health and Human Services for students preparing for careers in the health sciences.

Health Professions Student Loan (HPSL): A long-term, low-interest loan program designed to assist students in specific health profession disciplines.

HHS: *See Health and Human Services, U.S. Department of.*

Hope Scholarship: A federal tax credit for higher education expenses.

HPSL: *See Health Professions Student Loan.*

I

Income: Amount of money received from any or all of the following: wages, interest, dividends, sales or rental of property or services, business or farm profits, certain welfare programs, and subsistence allowances such as taxable and non-taxable Social Security benefits and child support.

Income Protection Allowance: An allowance against income for the basic costs of maintaining family members in the home. The allowance is based upon consumption and other cost estimates of the Bureau of Labor Statistics for a family at a low standard of living.

Independent Student: A student who: (a) will be 24 years of age by December 31 of the academic year in which the student seeks financial aid, or who (b) is an orphan or a ward of the court; (c) is a veteran; (d) is married or is a graduate or professional student; (e) has legal dependents other than a spouse; or (f) presents documentation of other unusual circumstances demonstrating independence to the student financial aid administrator.

Institutional Costs: Charges for tuition, fees, institutionally owned or operated room and board, and other educationally related charges assessed by the institution.

Institutional Student Information Record (ISIR): Output document or information that a school receives by participating in the electronic data exchange process. Contains the results of the FAFSA a student filed, whether it was filed on paper or electronically. Electronic version of the Student Aid Report (SAR). *Also see Student Aid Report.*

Investment Plans: Educational savings programs, usually sponsored by commercial banking institutions.

ISIR: *See Institutional Student Information Record.*

L

Legal Dependent: A biological or adopted child, or a person for whom the applicant has been appointed legal guardian, and for whom the applicant provides more than half support. In addition, a person who lives with and receives at least half support from the applicant and will continue to receive that support during the award year. (Note: For the FAFSA, only the natural or adoptive parent(s) should complete the form.)

Legal Resident: A person who has met a state or local district's requirements for being declared a resident. May also refer to an individual who is not a U.S. citizen but is still eligible for federal financial aid funds. *Also see Eligible Noncitizen and Residency Requirement.*

Lifetime Learning Tax Credit: A federal tax credit for higher education expenses.

Loan: An advance of funds that is evidenced by a promissory note requiring the recipient to repay the specified amount(s) under prescribed conditions.

Loan Forgiveness: Refers to the cancellation of a portion—or all—of an education loan in exchange for the borrower meeting specified criteria.

Loan Repayment Program: A special program available to qualified students who have attended college on federally funded student loans and who subsequently enlist in the Army for at least three years in a job specialty.

M

Merit-Based Aid: Student assistance awarded because of a student's achievement or talent in a particular area, such as academics, athletics, music, etc.

Methodology: Refers to the system used to calculate the Expected Family Contribution (i.e., the Federal Need Analysis Methodology).

Military Scholarships: Reserve Officer Training Corps (ROTC) scholarships available for the Army, Navy, and Air Force at many colleges and universities throughout the United States. These scholarships cover tuition, fees, books, and supplies and include a subsistence allowance.

Montgomery G.I. Bill: A program to help military personnel pay for postsecondary education. Sometimes called the New G.I. Bill.

N

National and Community Service (AmeriCorps): A program established through the National and Community Service Trust Act of 1993 designed to reward individuals who provide community service with educational benefits and/or loan forgiveness or cancellation.

National Health Service Corps (NHSC) Scholarship: Scholarship program for students who pursue full-time courses of study in certain health profession disciplines, and are willing to serve as primary care practitioners in underserved areas after completing their education.

National SMART Grants: National Science and Mathematics Access to Retain Talent (SMART) Grants for up to $4,000 are available to U.S. citizens who are Federal Pell Grant recipients and enrolled full-time in a third- or fourth-year baccalaureate degree program in specified majors. Must maintain a 3.0 GPA and demonstrate financial need.

National Student Loan Data System (NSLDS): A national database of Title IV loan information and selected federal grant data.

Need: *See Financial Need.*

Need Analysis: A system by which an applicant's ability to pay for educational expenses is evaluated and calculated. Need analysis consists of two primary components: (a) determination of an estimate of the applicant's and/or family's ability to contribute to educational expenses; and (b) determination of an accurate estimate of the educational expenses themselves.

Need Analysis Formula: Defines the data elements used to calculate the Expected Family Contribution (EFC); there are two distinct formulas: regular and simplified. The formula determines the EFC under the Federal Need Analysis Methodology.

Need-Based Aid: Student assistance awarded because a student's financial circumstances would not permit him or her to afford the cost of a postsecondary education.

Need Equation: *See Financial Need Equation.*

Noninstitutional Costs: Costs associated with postsecondary attendance that are not assessed by the institution, such as off-campus room and board, books, supplies, transportation, and other miscellaneous personal expenses.

Non-Need-Based Aid: Aid based on criteria other than need, such as academic, musical, or athletic ability. Also refers to federal student aid programs where the Expected Family Contribution (EFC) is not part of the need equation.

Non-Resident Student: *See Out-of-State Student.*

Notification: *See Award Letter and Financial Aid Notification.*

Nursing Student Loan (NSL): Loans available to nursing students attending approved nursing schools offering a diploma or associate, baccalaureate, or graduate degree in nursing.

O

Out-of-State Student: As defined by a public institution, a student who is not a legal resident of the state or local district that is legislatively and fiscally responsible for supervision of that institution; generally, such students are assessed higher tuition rates than those for legal residents. Also referred to as non-resident students.

Overaward: A situation in which the student's combined resources, including Expected Family Contribution (EFC) and financial aid, are greater than the Cost of Attendance. Outside certain tolerance levels, overawards are not permitted for students receiving federal student assistance funds.

P

Packaging: The process of combining various types of student aid (grants, loans, scholarships, and employment) to attempt to meet full amount of student's need.

Packaging Philosophy: The postsecondary institution's rationale for combining different types of aid to meet a student's need. This varies from school to school.

Part-Time Student: One who attends an institution on a less-than-full-time basis as defined by the institution.

Portability: An attribute of certain student aid programs that allows an eligible student to receive funds from any eligible institution rather than one specific institution. Applies to Federal Pell Grants as well as to some state scholarships that students may use at postsecondary institutions, including those located outside the state awarding the funds.

Prepayment Penalty: The charge the lender assesses to borrowers who repay a loan faster than the maximum repayment period stated in the promissory note. Federal loan programs do not have prepayment penalties.

Prime Rate: The interest rate that banks charge to their most creditworthy customers. Alternative loan lenders may advertise "Prime plus 1 percent" or "Prime plus 0 percent," which means that your interest rate is variable, depending upon the fluctuations of the prime rate.

Principal: The amount of money borrowed through a loan; does not include interest or other charges, unless they are capitalized.

Privacy Acts: Those collective statutes that serve to protect an individual from the release of specified data without the individual's prior written consent.

Projected Year Income: Income expected to be received during the first calendar year of the award year; may also be some other 12-month period.

Promissory Note: The legal document that binds a borrower to the repayment obligations and other terms and conditions that govern a loan program.

R

Reauthorization: A Congressional review process intended to refine authorized federal programs to ensure they continue to meet the needs of the populations they are intended to serve.

Regular Student: A person who is enrolled or accepted for enrollment at an institution of higher education for the purpose of obtaining a degree, certificate, or other recognized educational credential offered by the institution.

Renewable Award: An award that does not need to be applied for each year.

Renewal FAFSA: One type of FAFSA that resembles a SAR and bears the same questions as the FAFSA. The Renewal FAFSA contains the student's prior year responses to certain data items that are likely to remain constant from year to year. Students are notified by e-mail or postcard to complete the Renewal FAFSA online.

Repayment Schedule: A plan that should be provided to the borrower at the time he or she ceases at least half-time study. The plan should set forth the principal and interest due on each installment and the number of payments required to pay the loan in full. In addition, it should include the interest rate, the due date of the first payment, and the frequency of payments.

Reserve Officer Training Corps Scholarship Program: *See ROTC Scholarship Program.*

Residency Requirement: Criteria students must meet to be considered residents of a state or district; used in some cases to determine tuition charges. *Also see Eligible Noncitizen and Legal Resident.*

Resources: Resources include, but are not limited to, any: (a) funds the student is entitled to receive from a Federal Pell Grant; (b) waiver of tuition and fees; (c) grants, including ACG, National SMART,

FSEOG and ROTC subsistence allowances; (d) scholarships, including athletic and ROTC scholarships; (e) need-based fellowships or assistantships; (f) insurance programs for the student's education; (g) long-term loans made by the institution, including Federal Perkins and Direct Loans; (h) earnings from need-based employment; (i) veterans benefits; and (j) any portion of other long-term loans, including Federal Stafford Loans, Federal PLUS Loans, state-sponsored, or private loans, not used as a substitute for the EFC.

ROTC Scholarship Program: Competitive scholarship that pays for tuition, fees, books, a monthly living stipend, and other benefits in exchange for participating in drills and classes during the academic year, military camp during the summer, and, upon graduation, full-time active duty in the military for at least four years.

S

SAR: *See Student Aid Report.*

SAR Information Acknowledgment: A non-correctable one-page Student Aid Report containing Part I only.

Satisfactory Academic Progress: The progress required of a financial aid recipient in acceptable studies or other activities to fulfill a specified educational objective. Students are usually evaluated once a year against a preset standard of credit or clock hours.

Scholarship: A form of financial assistance that does not require repayment or employment and is usually made to students who demonstrate or show potential for distinction, usually in academic or athletic performance or have other special talents.

Scholarship Search Services: Organizations that claim to help students find little-known and unused financial aid funds. Families who are interested in using such a service should carefully investigate the company first.

Scholarships for Disadvantaged Students (SDS): A federal scholarship program designed to assist disadvantaged students enrolled in certain health profession disciplines.

School Year: *See Academic Year.*

Self-Help Aid: Funds provided through the work and effort of the student, including savings from past earnings, income from current earnings, or a loan to be repaid from future earnings.

Self-Help Expectation: The assumption that a student has an obligation to help pay for a portion of his or her education.

Service Academy: The five postsecondary institutions administered by branches of the military (U.S. Military Academy, U.S. Air Force Academy, U.S. Naval Academy, U.S. Coast Guard Academy, and U.S. Merchant Marine Academy).

Simplified Needs Test: An alternate method of calculating the Expected Family Contribution for families with adjusted gross incomes of less than $50,000, who have filed, or are eligible to file, an IRS Form 1040A or 1040EZ, or are not required to file an income tax return. Also includes recipients of federal means-tested benefit programs. Excludes all assets from consideration.

Special Allowance: The payment the federal government provides to lenders to bring total interest rates up to market value; acts as an incentive to lending institutions to offer loans in the Federal Family Education Loan programs.

Specialized Training for Army Reserve Readiness (STARR): An educational program sponsored by the Army Reserve whereby the Reserve pays all education-related expenses for Reservists who train in selected medical specialties at their local colleges.

Statement of Educational Purpose: Statement signed by the student financial aid recipient indicating his or her agreement to use all financial aid funds awarded for educational or educationally related purposes only. Included as part of the FAFSA.

Student Aid Report (SAR): The official notification sent to a student as a result of the Central Processing System (CPS) receiving an applicant record (via FAFSA) for the student. The SAR summarizes applicant information, an Expected Family Contribution for the student, and displays other special messages related to the student's application. The SAR should be carefully reviewed for errors, and corrections should be submitted. In some instances, the SAR may need to be submitted to the financial aid office at the school the student plans to attend, but only if the school requests it. *Also see Institutional Student Information Record.*

Student Budget: *See Cost of Attendance.*

Student Contribution: A quantitative estimate of the student's ability to contribute to postsecondary expenses for a given year.

Subsidized Loan: A loan in which the federal government pays both the interest accrued while the borrower is enrolled in school at least half-time as well as the interest accrued during the six-month grace period following the borrower's last day of at least half-time enrollment.

T

Taxable Income: Income earned from wages, salaries, and tips, as well as interest income, dividend income, business or farm profits, and rental or property income.

Title IV Programs: Those federal student aid programs authorized under Title IV of the Higher Education Act of 1965, as amended. Includes: the Federal Pell Grant, Academic Competitiveness Grants, National SMART Grants, Federal Supplemental Educational Opportunity Grant, Federal Work-Study, Federal Perkins Loan, Federal Stafford Loan, Federal PLUS Loan, Federal Direct Loan, Federal Direct PLUS Loan, and LEAP.

Tuition Payment Plans: A strategy by which payment for present costs of postsecondary education is extended into a future period of time.

U

Undergraduate Student: A student who has not achieved the level of a baccalaureate or first-professional degree.

Unmet Need: The difference between a student's total Cost of Attendance at a specific institution and the student's total available resources.

Unsubsidized Loan: A loan in which the borrower is responsible for all interest payments, even while he or she is enrolled in school and during the grace period.

Untaxed Income: All income received that is not reported to the Internal Revenue Service or is reported but excluded from taxation. Such income would include, but not be limited to, any untaxed portion of Social Security benefits, Earned Income Credit, welfare payments, untaxed capital gains, interest on tax-free bonds, dividend exclusion, and military and other subsistence and quarters allowances.

V

Variable Interest Rate: An interest rate on a loan that is adjusted at regular intervals, such as monthly, quarterly, or yearly.

Verification: The process of confirming information submitted on the FAFSA through the comparison of specified documents to the data on the output document. Schools must verify data for students selected by the federal Central Processing System (CPS) following procedures established by regulation. Schools may also select additional applicants to undergo the verification process.

Verification Worksheet: The document the postsecondary institution sends to the student, to be completed by the student and his or her family, and returned to the institution, to obtain documentation of the verification.

Veteran (for the purposes of determining dependency): A person who has served on active duty in the Army, Navy, Air Force, Marines, or Coast Guard, or was a cadet or midshipman at one of the service academies (except Coast Guard), and who was discharged other than dishonorably. Students who are currently on active duty (other than for training) are also considered veterans for the FAFSA. Veterans are considered to be independent. There is no minimum length-of-service requirement.

Veterans Educational Benefits: Assistance programs for eligible veterans and/or their dependents for education or training.

Vocational Rehabilitation: Programs administered by state departments of vocational rehabilitation services to assist individuals who have a physical or mental disability that is a substantial handicap to employment.

W

William D. Ford Federal Direct Loan (Direct Loan) Program: The collective name for the Direct Loan (subsidized and unsubsidized), Direct PLUS Loan, and Direct Consolidation Loan programs. Loan funds for these programs are provided by the federal government to students and parents through postsecondary institutions that participate in the program. With the exception of certain repayment options, the terms and conditions of loans made under the Direct Loan Program are almost identical to those made under the FFEL Program.

Work-Study: A form of self-help aid that carries the obligation of work in order to receive the award. Employment can be both on- and off-campus.

NOTES

NOTES

NOTES

NOTES

NOTES

NOTES

NOTES